Buckinghamshire
MURDERS

DR JONATHAN OATES

The History Press

I would like to dedicate this book to my son, Benjamin.

First published 2012

The History Press
The Mill, Brimscombe Port
Stroud, Gloucestershire, GL5 2QG
www.thehistorypress.co.uk

© Dr Jonathan Oates, 2012

The right of Dr Jonathan Oates to be identified as the Author
of this work has been asserted in accordance with the
Copyrights, Designs and Patents Act 1988.

British Library Cataloguing in Publication Data.
A catalogue record for this book is available from the British Library.

ISBN 978 0 7524 7032 8

Typesetting and origination by The History Press
Printed in Great Britain

CONTENTS

Acknowledgements   5

Introduction   6

1.   The Toll House Murders   11
   Aston Clinton, 1822

2.   Accident or Murder?   23
   Tingewick, 1822

3.   Justice Delayed   28
   Aylesbury, 1828-1830

4.   Dreadful Murder at Dorney   43
   Dorney, 1853

5.   Massacre at Denham   57
   Denham, 1870

6.   A Domestic Murder   71
   Olney, 1873

7.   Dreadful Murder at Slough   78
   Slough, 1881

8.   Lucky Escape?   89
   Bledlow, 1893

9.   Child Murder at Colnbrook   97
   Colnbrook, 1900

10. The Second Slough Murder   105
    Slough, 1910

11. An Eton Murder   117
    Eton, 1912

12. A Double Murder   129
    Little Kimble, 1914

13. 'I have been a source of worry and trouble'   138
    Little Marlow, 1921

14. A Pub Shooting   149
    High Wycombe, 1937

    Afterword   156
    Bibliography   157
    Index   159

ACKNOWLEDGEMENTS

As always, I have to thank several people for their help in the production of this book. Paul Lang, for his assistance and helpful suggestions while proof reading, and for his generous lending of a number of postcards from his vast collection. Thanks to Michael Shaw, historian of the county police force, for the biographical information provided about a number of the officers who appear within these pages, and to both Ken Pearce and Jean Smith, each for supplying a picture to use in the book. And finally, to my wife, who accompanied me on a number of visits to parts of the county in order to take some of the photographs that appear in the book.

INTRODUCTION

It seems that fictional murders in Buckinghamshire are better known than real-life murders, as the many testimonies to the hugely popular television series *Midsomer Murders* show. However, there are some well-known criminals and crimes that are associated with the county. In 1933, for example, a man was arrested for the theft of a car in Twyford; it was two decades later that he was revealed to be the infamous John Reginald Halliday Christie, serial killer of 10 Rillington Place. It was in Buckinghamshire that, in 1963, clues to help apprehend the robbers of the Great Train Robbery were found, and it is where James Hanratty first accosted John Gregsten and Valerie Storrie, resulting in Gregsten's murder and Hanratty's execution in 1961. The corpse of Dennis Blakely, unfaithful lover of Ruth Ellis (the last woman to be hanged in England in 1955), and who was shot dead by her in Hampstead, was buried in Penn, Buckinghamshire. Florence Maybrick, who poisoned her husband (suspected by some as being Jack the Ripper) in 1889, was once incarcerated at Aylesbury Prison. Finally, it was in a hospital in Slough that the once feared London gangster, Ronnie Kray, died in 1995.

This collection, however, brings together only the most notorious of crimes; that of murder, and those which occurred in the county – including Slough, which, until the 1970s, was a part of Buckinghamshire. Focusing on the period between 1822 and 1937, fourteen capital crimes have been selected throughout these decades, though this is by no means a complete catalogue of the county's murders within these dates.

Hughenden Manor House. (Courtesy of Paul Lang)

The county is the eighth smallest of the thirty-nine English counties. In 1831, it had a population of 130,982, and in 1911 this had grown to 229,551. Some of this population growth may have been due to the introduction of the railway lines in the 1830s and '40s. These included the Great Western line to the south of the county, the North Western line, and the Great Western and Great Central Joint Railway (employees of which were involved in the murder related in chapter 12). In the nineteenth century, Buckinghamshire was, primarily, an agricultural county with very few industries; claiming wheat, barley, clover, pigs, sheep and cows as its main products. The few industries it did have, however, included lace, straw plaiting, paper mills and a shoe industry. There were few large towns, aside from Aylesbury and High Wycombe, and later, Slough, and the county was chiefly rural. There were a number of country houses, such as Hughenden Manor, once home to Victorian Prime Minister, Benjamin Disraeli, and West Wycombe Park, home of the Dashwoods.

There was no county-wide police force in Buckinghamshire until 1857. Prior to that, there were two chief forces employed to deal with crime. Firstly there were the parish constables, men selected every year from among their fellow parishioners. They were called upon to arrest criminals and escort them to the gaol and courts, but also dealt with other parish business, such as the implementation of the Poor Law. The second force was the Bow Street Runner.

The old gaol, Buckingham. (Courtesy of Paul Lang)

Founded in the eighteenth century, they were initially a very small force of paid thief takers in London, overseen by Henry Fielding and his blind half-brother, John. Their numbers and scope increased as time went by, so that by the early nineteenth century they were composed of both foot and horse patrols, and their remit extended for miles outside the metropolis.

By 1829, the Metropolitan Police had been formed, and although they were at first restricted to London, by 1839 their jurisdiction had spread to adjoining counties. The 1839 Police Act enabled counties and boroughs to establish their own police forces, consisting of blue-uniformed civilians, who were to act as a visible deterrent to crime as well as to apprehend criminals. These were unpopular at first, suspected as being detrimental to civil liberty and a drain on taxes. The 1839 Act was not compulsory, however, and some counties decided not to implement it; Buckinghamshire being one.

However, the County and Borough Police Act of 1856 made the establishment of police forces obligatory throughout England, and it was in 1857 that the Buckinghamshire constabulary was first established. It was made up of a chief constable, seven superintendents (one of whom was the deputy chief constable), seven inspectors, twenty-nine sergeants and 184 constables. There were ninety-two police stations in the county in total, most of which were run by a single constable.

The county police were initially under the control of the county quarter sessions of magistrates, but following the formation of the county council in 1888, a standing joint committee of both councillors and magistrates was formed in order to oversee police policy and activity. There was also a separate High Wycombe constabulary who operated in tandem to the county force, with both forces having a police station in the same town. In 1968 the force came to an end, being merged with the Berkshire and Oxfordshire forces to form the Thames Valley Police Force, of which the fictional character Inspector Morse is a well-known member.

The sources used for this book are primarily newspapers, both national, such as *The Times* and the *Morning Chronicle*, and local, such as the *Slough Express* and various other Buckinghamshire newspapers. I have also used sources well-known to the genealogist, such as census returns, civil registration records, directories, wills, and army records in order to flesh out the characters who appear within the pages of the book.

The author was born in Buckinghamshire; Amersham to be exact. This is his tenth book about true crime, chiefly from the nineteenth and twentieth centuries.

Dr Jonathan Oates, 2012

1

THE TOLL HOUSE MURDERS

Aston Clinton, 1822

During the eighteenth century, the introduction of turnpike trusts ensured the improvement of the roads in Britain. Work was financed by payments levied on horse-drawn traffic, and these monies were collected by toll-house keepers, who were accommodated in houses by the sides of roads. Initially, these new tolls were met with hostility, and on occasion toll-house keepers and their houses were attacked. By the nineteenth century they had become less novel and were more accepted by travellers. Yet, for one couple who collected tolls in Buckinghamshire, there was another danger – not irate travellers or angry mobs, but a more universal and deadly foe – itinerant thieves who were prepared to use violence in the pursuit of what they wanted. Toll houses were very attractive for thieves, as, quite often, they were isolated from other dwellings and contained substantial amounts of money which had been collected from travellers. Theft and murder were both punishable by death at this time, and, more often than not, the thieves would kill anyone who might be able to identify them.

On Tuesday, 19 November 1822, an aged couple, Rachel and Edward Needle, were killed at their toll house at Aston Clinton, a couple of miles outside of Aylesbury. Little is known about the couple, but they were rumoured to have amassed some considerable savings. They had been quite well earlier on in the day, for Mrs Fanny Norris had had tea with them between three and five o'clock that afternoon, and later, Charles White recalled conversing with Mr Needle. Joseph Davies was the first to discover the crime. At just before quarter past six the following morning, he was on his way to fetch his master's horse, which was in the field adjoining the toll house. He passed the gate and saw that the door was open. He thought this was odd, because he passed the door every day and usually saw Mr Needle there. He took a quick look in and saw Rachel's body lying in the first room. Shocked and scared, he raised the alarm immediately. The first person he saw was the proprietor of the Aylesbury coach, James Wyatt, who was stopping by the toll gate. Wyatt went into the house and found Rachel's body on the floor of the sitting room and her husband's body in their bed, covered with a sheet.

William Hayward, an Aylesbury surgeon, was summoned to the scene. He arrived between nine and ten that morning, along with John Blissett, his assistant. Rachel's body was bruised and bloody. He thought that she and her husband, who was unclothed, had been killed by the edge of a blunt instrument or bludgeon, as they had both suffered severe injuries to the head. In detail, Mr Needle had a fracture on the right side of his skull, and over his right eye a wound that was an inch long and half-an-inch deep. His right ear was lacerated and torn and there were marks on his right hand, as though he had tried to ward off the blows. In both cases, the blows to the head had been the likely cause of death. Joseph Hill, an Aylesbury shoemaker, arrived not long after Joseph Davies, and raised the alarm, and located the bludgeons used to commit the murder – one of which was under the bed. They were bloody and one was almost broken in the middle.

The day after the bodies were discovered, the Magistrates' Marylebone Office received details of the murders. The principal investigator was a Mr Minshull, a Bow Street Runner who lived in Aylesbury. On being told of the murders, he went to the crime scene accompanied by many countrymen, who he had sworn in as special constables. They were sent in all directions from the murder scene, with instructions to apprehend any suspicious person they might meet. Minshull also sent messages to all resident magistrates in the neighbourhood, asking for their co-operation. These included the Earl of Bridgewater, whose seat was near Berkhamsted, and because he was absent, the message arrived in the hands of his secretary, Mr Atty, who went to the nearest village, Gaddesden, to inform the residents of the contents of the message.

Meanwhile, at about eight in the evening, some of the men despatched by Minshull arrived at the Bridgewater Arms in Little Gaddesden, around the same time as those summoned by Atty. Mr Bennett, the publican, upon being told the cause of alarm, said that there were three strangers in his tap room – two men and a woman – whom he believed were acting suspiciously. Joseph Impey, an ostler at the pub, noted that they were exhausted on arrival. They then ate beef

The Bridgewater Arms, Little Gaddesden.

steaks, recently purchased from a butcher in the village, which they had paid for with half pennies. They also carried bundles with them and on being observed, the woman retired to the toilets. The three were apprehended and detained by William Clarke and William Martin, the two constables for Tring. It was now half past nine at night.

They found bloodstains on the elbow and cuffs of one of the men's jackets, which was wet and dirty, as if attempts had been recently made to wash the blood off. Clay and dirt had been used to try and conceal other incriminating marks. There was also blood on a handkerchief and one of the bags they had with them.

Unbeknown to the constables, the first man arrested on suspicion of the crime was James Richards, described as a stout athletic countryman, and who had been detained on the day after the murder. Earlier that day he had been in The Sign of the Lord Thorley pub, in London, when a man was reading an account of the murders. Richards' face blanched and he appeared agitated. In a very hurried manner he asked where the crime had been committed, and soon afterwards asked directions to Fleet Street. Another customer in the pub thought that his behaviour was suspicious and reported it to the magistrates, with the result that Richards was taken into custody and questioned.

Richards said that he was from Oxfordshire. He had travelled from North Wales to Salisbury, then to Southampton and to Guildford, and then arrived in London. He claimed ignorance of the murders prior to hearing about them being read aloud in the pub. He added that he had two brothers living in London, but had not seen them since last spring and did not know where they lived. He was then detained until further enquiries into the case were made, but, presumably, was released as soon as news came from Minshull.

Meanwhile, the rector of Little Gaddesden, Revd James Horseman, the Earl of Bridgewater and Revd Mr Robert Jenks of Berkhamsted, all of whom were magistrates, arrived in Little Gaddesden. They examined the prisoners separately. Their suspicions surrounding the murder were confirmed when all three of the prisoners' stories contradicted the others. Proclaiming his innocence, the first prisoner told them that he was a shoemaker from Leicester who had been traipsing the country for work, and that he had only just met his companion on that very day. However, when the keeper of the county gaol at Aylesbury, James Sheriff, arrived, he said that he recognised the three prisoners after he had seen them lurking around the locality for some days. This led to the magistrates' suspicions being lent additional weight.

The prisoners gave their names as James Croker, Thomas Randall and Martha Barnacle. Their bundles were examined and found to contain items which had been stolen from the toll house, including a pair of worsted stockings, a pair of leather braces, a large clasp knife, a pair of leather gloves, a pair of shoes, a tobacco stopper, 12s 6d in silver and four pence. There had been little physical evidence left in the toll house, but some nails, which matched those on the prisoners' boots, were found there.

The following day, Martha was questioned alone. She said that she had known Thomas Randall for about a year but had only known the other for only a short while. On the night of the murder, all three had been together at Berkhamsted. The men left at eight that night, telling her that they were going to do a job which would fetch a hundred pounds. She claimed that she then exhorted them to not commit murder, before arranging to meet the next day at an appointed place, before stating to the magistrates that she had been told not 'to tell all she knew, lest she be murdered herself,' so she said no more.

Further investigations continued on the Friday following the murder, at the King's Arms at Berkhamsted. At four that afternoon, the prisoners were taken to Aylesbury. En route they stopped at the toll house where the murders had been committed. The two men were taken separately into the rooms where the bodies had been found; Croker was first to enter and once they were both inside

The King's Arms, Berkhamsted.

Aylesbury Convict Prison. (Courtesy of Paul Lang)

they were shown the corpses, which were in their coffins. Croker patently did not want to view them and remained silent. Randall, however, did look and said that it was a dreadful spectacle, before thanking God that he had had no hand in their deaths. From their reactions, the investigators believed that it had been Croker who had inflicted the fatal wounds.

It was later discovered that a horse had been taken from an adjoining field and brought to the gate. Mrs Needle, believing this was a traveller arriving at the gate, went to the door of the toll house and then went into the road. Although her body had been found inside the house, the amount of mud attached to her clothes suggested that she had been killed outside and dragged inside afterwards, to delay the discovery of the crime.

Earlier that day, the inquest had been opened at The White Hart in Aylesbury, before John Chersley, the county coroner. Reverend Messrs Ashfield and Revd Thomas Archer, vicar of Whitchurch (both of whom were magistrates) were present, and the jury was composed of a dozen respectable farmers and inhabitants of the town of Aylesbury.

After Hayward gave evidence regarding the method of the murders, and hearing Davies' evidence of finding the bodies, Charles Finch gave a rather more lengthy statement. He was a labourer who lived in Aston Clinton, and at 10.30 on the Monday night he was working near to the Aston turnpike. He saw two men on the road nearby (later identified as Croker and Randall). One was a short, thick man carrying a bundle under his arm. He was wearing a light-coloured, drab cloth coat, with light, worsted cord breeches which came over the calves of his legs, and a single-breasted coat. He said that the man had had a pale face. The other was a tall, slightly lame man who was wearing a light-coloured fustian frock coat and carrying a black thorn stick. He wore ankle boots and was dark-looking. Finch thought they were behaving oddly as they left the road and moved through a field towards the toll house. At five o'clock the next morning he saw the two men again, and once more that night, at about half past ten. On the second occasion they were wearing the same clothes as before, and this time they had a woman with them. Finch thought that they looked like ruffians and said to his companion, 'I should not like to meet them on a dark night.' They were walking towards Aston Clinton at this time.

Mrs Norris, a friend of the Needles, was shown items which had been found on the three suspects. This included a pipe-stopper, which was made of copper and plated with silver. Mrs Norris was convinced that this had belonged to the Needles. There were shoes and stockings among the stolen items, which she believed may have been owned by the elderly couple, but she could not be entirely sure about those. The inquest was adjourned until Saturday evening.

William Wood of Aston Clinton, a cobbler and an old friend of the Needles, was examined next. He was shown the shoes that the prisoners claimed belonged to them, but Wood was convinced that they had belonged to his late friend and stated that he had examined the shoes on the Sunday before the murders. Thomas Wyatt, a Tring constable, recalled meeting the prisoners on the road, walking rapidly towards Tring in the early hours of Wednesday morning.

The coroner summed up the proceedings with great perspicuity. At half past nine he concluded, and the jury only took a short time to decide their verdict. They declared that Thomas Randall and James Croker were guilty of wilful murder, and that they were to stand trial at the next assizes.

In the meantime, the Needles were buried at St Michael's Church, with the funeral expenses being met by their former employers, the trustees of the turnpike.

Later that month, a man named Rowe, who lived near Tring, was examined by the magistrates. He claimed that he had seen the three prisoners together on the evening of the murder. According to him, Croker had said that they had a

St Michael's churchyard, Aston Clinton, where Mr and Mrs Needle are buried.

job to do, and were afraid they would be too late, before leaving the pub. On the Thursday following the crime, Rowe had found two bundles under a hedge on the road from Tring to Little Gaddesden. In these were a pistol – identified as belonging to Mr Needle – some of Mrs Needle's clothing, two silver spoons and other items belonging to the murdered couple. Some suspected Rowe of being involved with the murders, as he had been drinking with the accused prior to the crime. He was questioned regarding his movements on the fatal night, and how it was that he had made the discovery of the bundles – fortunately for him, he was able to satisfactorily defend himself against both accusations and was discharged.

Randall and Croker stood trial at the Spring Assizes, held at Aylesbury on 4 March 1823. Such was the interest in the case, that people started gathering at half past eight in the morning and, by nine o'clock, the courtroom was crowded. Randall pleaded not guilty, whereas Croker pleaded guilty. Croker was told by the judge that he should withdraw his plea and change it to that of his associate; otherwise he would not receive a trial but an automatic verdict of guilty. Croker did not change his mind and only Randall was tried, with Croker sitting through it.

Charles White was the first witness to be called. He stated that he had passed through the turnpike gates at between nine and ten on Tuesday night, and at that time Needle was alive and well. He then said that he had found the corpses the following morning.

Mrs Todd, a lodging-house keeper in Walton Green, Aylesbury, said that Randall had stayed with her on the Saturday preceding the murders. Croker had arrived on Sunday and all three stayed there on the Sunday night. They stayed on Monday night, too, but all left at nine o'clock the following morning. Francis Cook of Berkhamsted, another lodging-house keeper, recalled Randall arriving there on Tuesday afternoon and said that Martha Barnacle had slept there alone. Randall arrived to collect her the following morning at seven, telling her that Croker had gone on to Hunton Bridge, about nine miles away, and that they should follow him and breakfast on the road.

Mary Tomkins, landlady of The Green Man in Tring, recalled the three drinking there between ten and eleven on the morning before the murders. Croker remained there all day, but the other two left. After they had returned, and before they headed out again, she recalled one of them saying, 'It is a quarter past – half past eight is our time, and that will be soon enough.' Thomas Monk then told the court that he saw the two on the road to Aylesbury after leaving the pub.

Martha Barnacle, a single woman from Cubbington, Warwickshire, then gave her evidence. She and Randall had been traipsing the countryside during November 1822, selling cottons and laces. She had met him at Foster's Booth, near Towcester in Northamptonshire. He was on his way to London and promised he would marry her on arrival. They travelled to Buckinghamshire and met Croker. Once they had arrived in Aylesbury, Croker said he was going to Oxford, but Martha begged Randall not to accompany him as she thought he was bad company. Randall replied that he was off to Tring instead, to sell a greatcoat. The two men returned that evening, with food and four gowns – the latter had been 'found' between Tring and Aylesbury. Randall told her that he knew a girl with £100 who wanted to run away with him. He said he was not in love with her, but that they could relieve her of her money, though Martha begged him not to do so.

On the following day, the three left Aylesbury for Berkhamsted, and along the way they retrieved some goods that Randall had hidden behind a hedge. They then went to The Green Man at Tring. Randall and Martha left to go to a lodging house in Berkhamsted, where he left her. He returned on the Wednesday morning, and, despite Martha urging that they eat breakfast there, insisted on leaving immediately. She thought they would be travelling to London but he said they would not, as there were bundles they had to collect, which he had hidden near Berkhamsted. She asked if they had the £100 he had spoken of, to which he replied, 'No, we have had a very bad night of it,' but he did confirm that they had enough to get them to London. They eventually met Croker and ate breakfast, before proceeding to Gaddesden.

Various witnesses confirmed that the goods found on the prisoners had belonged to the Needles. The evidence against Randall seemed clear enough. The judge had no doubt that Randall was guilty and summed up the case, pointing out the glaring evidence against him and the horror of the crime. He said it did not matter whether Randall had struck both, or either of the Needles, or had merely watched whilst it was being done; either was a capital crime. The jury returned a guilty verdict and Randall was asked if he had anything to say about the verdict, to which he replied that he did not. He then asked if the money which was on his person when he was arrested could be returned to him, and was told that if it were lawfully his, it would be.

The judge then passed the death sentence on both Randall and Croker. He directed that after their deaths, the bodies would be delivered to medical schools for the purpose of dissection. He then entreated the condemned men to prepare their souls for another world. He thought that Croker, because of his admission of guilt, had already begun the process of recommending his soul to his maker, but said that Randall should now admit his guilt. Sentence would be carried out in two days' time. Croker bowed to the judge and thanked him for his words towards them.

The day after the trial, Randall asked to see Martha, which the magistrates allowed. However, the clergymen opposed this, claiming it would distract and unnerve Randall too much, so the meeting was postponed until eleven that night. The two met, and despite her role in condemning him by appearing as a witness, the meeting was tender and affectionate; all of Randall's earlier anger against her having dissipated. Indeed, it transpired that the money he had asked about was a gift for Martha.

That night, Revd Dr George Scobell, vicar of Turville, sat with the prisoners, praying and offering spiritual consolation. The prison chaplain, the Revd Archer, and Scobell, heard their confessions, in which more was learnt about the men's backgrounds.

Croker had been born in Langford Butfield, in Somerset. His father, a bricklayer and a widower, looked after him and his four brothers and four sisters. Croker had worked with his father until his late teens, then left for Bristol to work as an apprentice to his brother-in-law, who was a baker. He stayed with him for four years and then took another master as a journeyman, before switching to a number of other employers. On 4 March 1818 he married, but separated from his wife after three years, apparently because he became tired of her wild habits. He then left Bristol for London and was employed as a journeyman baker. In October 1822, he left the capital, fell in with Randall and embarked on a short crime spree.

It was learnt that Randall had also gone by the name of John Bryan. He had been born in Stockton, Warwickshire, in about 1798. His parents were now both dead, but he had a sister who had lived in Staffordshire. Randall began working for a farmer when he was nine or ten and stayed there until his teens. His downfall began when he went to Birmingham, where he fell in with bad company. He picked pockets and robbed houses, but on the cusp of being caught, he left the district. In 1819, he stood trial at the local assizes but was acquitted. He then went to Leicestershire, where he committed many acts of pickpocketing, before committing burglary in Gaddesby and Queensborough. With regard to his final crime, Randall said that Croker had persuaded him that there would be rich pickings at the toll house, and that it was not he who struck the fatal blows.

Before his time on Earth ended, Randall wrote to his uncle:

My dear and honoured Uncle,

These are the last words you will ever receive from your unhappy and afflicted nephew. You have long been informed of my miserable condition in this place, to which I have now to add that yesterday was the awful day of trial, and after a long and patient hearing, before a kind judge and an impartial jury, I was convicted of the dreadful crime of murder. My guilt was manifest to a crowded Court, my sentence was just and tomorrow morning, soon after the sun has risen, I shall undergo the tremendous judgement of the offended laws of my country. May God almighty enable me to undergo, with fortitude and resignation, my terrible fate, and may my example be some atonement for the bloody violence of which I have been guilty! Stained with the blood of two innocent victims of my cruelty, where can I turn for mercy? How can I expect pardon and forgiveness for so heinous a crime? My case, I trust, is not altogether hopeless. In this place of confinement I have had opportunities of religious instruction, which, during the latter part of my life, I despised. From the comforts of religion, I and my fellow criminal feel our souls refreshed; amidst the sorrow and disgrace which my ignominious fate will bring upon you and the rest of my family, it will afford you some consolation to know that God has graciously enabled me to sustain my soul with wonderful fortitude. And I rely on the same Almighty Power to support me in the bitter trial, which in a few short moments I must encounter. Of this I beg to assure you, with all sincerity, that even in this time of suffering I feel more real happiness than walked uninterrupted in the paths of sin and wickedness. I must devote the few short moments that remain to finish my account with my Maker and Redeemer. You will be kind enough to communicate the contents of this letter to all my relations. May God shower his blessings upon you in this world, and grant you everlasting life in that which is to come! So, prays, in this latest hours of his life, your guilty and afflicted, but not forsaken, nephew,

John Bryan

On the morning of Thursday 6 March, gallows were erected outside Aylesbury Prison. Long before the two men appeared, a multitude of spectators arrived, for public executions were entertainment as well as grim educational warnings. People aimed to be able to get the best view of the drama. At a few minutes past eight, Croker and Randall mounted the platform with firm steps. Croker addressed the crowd briefly, saying, 'May God bless you.' The caps were placed over the condemned men's heads before they were launched into oblivion. After they had hung there for an hour, they were cut down and their corpses sent to an anatomy school in London.

It seems that the crime happened thus: Croker and Randall were two itinerant burglars, who had spied out the relatively isolated premises which they intended to steal from, believing there would be rich pickings there. However, they were rather conspicuous in doing so. Arming themselves beforehand, they decoyed Mrs Needle to the turnpike gate and killed her there, before entering the premises to kill her husband and then loot the place at leisure. Leaving their weapons behind, they fled with what they could, but did not go far. Had they continued in their flight they may well have escaped the rudimentary methods of the law, but carelessness undid them. Whilst stopping at Gaddesden for food, they were overtaken; the goods in their possession and plenty of witnesses were enough to condemn them to death.

2

ACCIDENT OR MURDER?

Tingewick, 1822

On the evening of Monday, 25 November 1822, William Wells, publican of The Angel Inn, Buckingham, was found dead on the road near Tingewick. Newspaper reports gave the verdict at the inquest as either accident or murder – certainly no one ever seems to have been charged with his death, though one man stands out as a potential suspect.

Wells and a man named Benjamin Brewerton had been at a meeting about the turnpike trust at Banbury on the 25th. They then left for home, but Wells never arrived.

On the same night, Charles Cross, a Tingewick shoemaker, was on his way home from Buckingham, accompanied by his apprentice, John Durrant. At about half past nine, they were approaching the turnpike gate, which stood on the west side of Tingewick, when they saw a gig and horse without any occupant. Closer to the village itself, they made a rather more shocking discovery. By the side of the road was a man's body, with bloodstains underneath the head and on the roadway – he was dead.

Cross went to the turnpike gate, about 200 yards away, and found the turnpike keeper, Thomas Brewerton (father of Benjamin), and asked him whether a gig had recently passed that way. Thomas Brewerton confirmed that it had, about half an hour ago, and that Wells had been the occupant. Cross then went to the village to sound the alarm, and his apprentice called on Benjamin Brewerton, who he found sitting by his fireside with his wife. Upon hearing the news, Brewerton ran in an alarmed state towards where the corpse lay. Susanna Stokes, the toll-house keeper, called out to him but he did not answer. She then called out to him again,

The Angel Inn, Buckingham.

Toll house, Tingewick.

but still he didn't seem to have heard her, and carried on running away from the toll house, so she followed him. Cross soon joined her and before long all three were standing around the body. Brewerton had arrived first and was examining Wells' head. Once other people began to arrive, Cross decided to leave the scene.

One of the first men on the scene was the Clerk of Tingewick, Revd John Risley. Earlier that evening, he and Richard Steele, his servant, had been travelling back from Buckingham, and sometime between nine and ten had seen the master-less gig and horse. Benjamin Brewerton told the vicar that he had accompanied Wells back from Banbury, and that they had stopped at the Red Lion pub at Finmere en route. He said that they had quarrelled, but that Wells was not drunk and that he had no idea as to how Wells had died.

At 10.30 p.m., William Stone, a surgeon from Buckingham, arrived. He noted the position of the corpse before having it taken to the nearest inn, where he carried out a post-mortem for the benefit of the inevitable inquest. The next day, he made a proper examination in the presence of the coroner's jury. Both ears had been lacerated and there were wounds on the right cheek and chin, the upper lip was swollen and a tooth was missing. There was also a wound on the back of the right hand, as though Wells had tried to protect himself from the attack. There was a fracture to the skull near the ear, and Stone opened up the head to examine the brain for any damage.

The Red Lion pub, Finmere.

On the previous night he had examined the victim's clothing and found £3 1*s* 9*d* in his pockets – a not insubstantial sum. It appeared, therefore, that he had not been robbed, for he had just a shilling or two more than this amount when he departed for Banbury early on Monday morning.

There was much discussion about the nature of the quarrel between Wells and Brewerton. Earlier that night, Joseph Terry, a Tingewick labourer, had overheard Brewerton say, 'Damn his eyes, he shall have it,' as he was walking towards the turnpike earlier that evening, after having left home.

It seems that Wells and Brewerton had been at the pub between about six and seven o'clock. Mary Manstell, the publican's wife, recalled that the two men entered the tap room and drank two pints of ale and two-and-a-half quarters of gin. They seemed friendly at first, but then argued about money. Brewerton threatened to knock Wells' teeth down his throat. Mary intervened and the violence subsided. The two men then left for the gig, apparently friends once more. A few minutes later, they were back in the pub. Wells said, 'I don't know what to make of this fellow: he wants to fall out with me on the road,' to which Brewerton replied, 'It was only for fun.' Then Wells left again, planning to go to the gig and travel on alone, but he was followed almost immediately by Brewerton.

Later that evening, at about eight, Wells called on James Halton, butcher of Tingewick. He told the butcher that he had travelled from Banbury and that he had had a quarrel with Brewerton, firstly on the road and then at the Red Lion, before calling a truce and shaking hands. He then told him that they had then gone to the gig, where Brewerton was again abusive and threatening to fight him, before they returned to the pub and he left, alone. Halton thought that Wells was tipsy, but rational.

But what were Brewerton's precise movements on Monday night? Edmund Side, a labourer, had been at Brewerton's house for much of the evening, from six to nine. He thought that Brewerton arrived at 7.45 p.m., but only remained there for about five minutes, before leaving in the direction of the toll house. He was gone for fifteen minutes. Brewerton claimed that he had argued with both his wife and Wells, though presumably not at the same time, and it is not certain how recent these quarrels were. Susanna Stokes recalled seeing him arrive at the toll house at 8.30 p.m., and that he seemed drunk. There was a conversation between father and son; the latter saying that he had travelled with Wells. Susanna had Sarah Bedford fetch Brewerton's wife. She came and the two went home. However, Brewerton soon returned to the toll house, alone, and he argued with Susanna over family matters. He was said to have been causing a disturbance, so his brother John was called to fetch him; they were later seen together, drinking beer until about ten. Susanna recalled that at about at nine, Wells went through the turnpike gate on his gig.

The inquest took place on Wednesday, with Mr Burnham, the coroner, presiding. The jury were obliged to see the body again. The coroner directed them to return a verdict of accidental death, and this is what they did. However, some newspaper reports contradicted this, claiming a verdict of murder, but then there were further reports that this was mistaken and the original version held. If this was an accident, it must be presumed that either Wells fell from his gig and was killed by his own horse and cart, or that he was killed by another vehicle. No weapon was ever found. Unfortunately, the surgeon does not seem to have made a pronouncement on how Wells met his death. The wounds he outlined could have been made by a horse and gig, but they could also have been made by another human being. If the latter was the case, then the obvious suspect is Benjamin Brewerton, who had recently quarrelled with the deceased and was certainly in the vicinity at the right time, creating both motive and opportunity. Possibly Brewerton's drunken state had led him to kill Wells following their quarrel. It is certainly odd that Brewerton rushed to the scene of the crime as soon as he had heard, and that he was the first to arrive; also that he immediately told the vicar that he had been with Wells earlier in the evening, that they had quarrelled and that he was innocent.

Unfortunately, there are many questions that remain unanswered. What was it exactly that Wells and Brewerton were arguing about? We only know that it was about money. What were the relations between the two men? Was Susanna and Brewerton's quarrel relevant to Wells' death? Were Brewerton's brother and father involved in any way? The answers will never be known, but the questions are worth pondering.

3

JUSTICE DELAYED

Aylesbury, 1828–1830

Asenior Victorian detective declared that if the guilty party is not apprehended within twenty-four hours of a crime, it is likely that he will escape
detection. In more recent years there have been instances, often due to forensic advances, which have meant that killers have been brought to justice years
after committing their crime. In earlier times, this was far less common. To have
killed without witnesses and to have escaped without leaving clues or having
fallen under suspicion, usually meant that a murder would go unsolved and
the perpetrator would walk free. This case, however, was the exception which
proved the rule.

On Saturday, 25 October 1828, between two and three o'clock in the
afternoon, William Edden was seen at the top of Walton Street, Aylesbury.
Edden, or Heydon, was almost seventy years old, but was stout and hearty, and
about 6ft tall. He lived in Thame where he was a market gardener. Often he and
his son would take their produce to the market in Aylesbury. He was carrying
a sack of potatoes, and told Thomas Walker that he had hoped for 13*s* but had
only received 3*s*. Edden went to John Search at the wharf in Aylesbury, for coal.
He said he could not pay for it then as he only had a note for £20, but did offer to
write him a cheque for the amount required.

Edden went to The Ship pub at about three o'clock. Mrs Fountain, the
publican's wife, recalled him drinking a pint or two of beer and treating other
men to gin. He did not seem drunk, but could not pay because, as he said, he
only had a £20 note with him. He was then seen at The Rising Sun pub at about
half past four. Thomas Bass, a lollipop maker, was relaxing with Edden, who

The Rising Sun pub, Slough.

may have been a little tipsy by this point, over a glass of beer. When he left, Edden asked Bass if he could come with him to help guide the horse and cart.

They travelled together for a while, leaving Aylesbury along the Oxford Road, westwards, stopping at The Bugle Horn pub at Hartmill en route. Upon reaching The Castle pub, Edden got off the cart for a necessary purpose. Whilst getting off the cart his foot slipped, but he did not fall, and he carried on walking beside the cart for a mile. When they reached the crossroads near Haddenham, Edden said, 'This was the very spot where the attempt was made to rob me.' This had happened almost a year ago, but Bass did not know whom Edden suspected of being involved. Bass told him not to worry and the two men parted. It was about six o'clock at this point.

Between seven and eight that night, William King, a straw plait dealer, was travelling between Thame and Aylesbury with his thirteen-year-old son, Thomas. He recalled:

> I saw a cart on the road, without a horse. I asked my little boy, who was with me, what he saw, and he said, pointing to the ground, 'Here lies the harness.' I asked

him to look into the hind part of the cart, and tell me what was in it; he replied that whatever it was looked like a tree. I then asked him to go up and we proceeded in my cart about a quarter of a mile and there we saw something lying on the road. I hollowed out, 'Who is there?' and the only answer I got was a cry of 'Oh', or something of that sort: he appeared to me to be lying on his side.

William did not get out of his own cart and nor did he seem to have investigated closely, so did not help the man. Instead, he proceeded along the road and soon met some men and a cart coming towards him and his son. He told them about the man lying in the road and warned them not to run him over. He then carried on until he reached The Gibraltar pub. Everyone was in bed, except some women, and he told them there was a man and a cart in the road nearby.

Henry Taylor of Netley Mills also saw Edden that evening. He recalled, 'I asked who he was, twice or thrice, but received no answer. Being alone, I thought it was a trap laid for me, and was afraid to alight from my horse. I accordingly went on.' He later saw two men wearing black hats standing by the cart, which was about a quarter of a mile away. He returned home soon afterwards and told Edward Dodwell, his servant, what he had seen. The two of them, armed with pistols, returned to the scene. Taylor also took a sword with him. He stated:

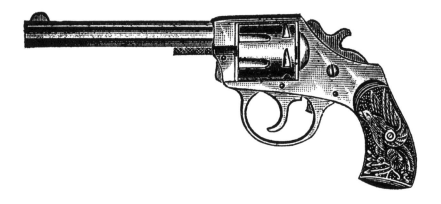

The Bugle Horn pub, Hartmill.

The Green Dragon pub, Haddenham.

Upon returning, my objective was to ascertain who the person lying in the road was, whether a person lying in wait, or one who had been murdered. He was in the same position as before, about a quarter of a mile from the cart. I do not think he had moved in the interval. When I got up to him I found him quite dead. I took hold of his arm and tried to move him, but he was quite insensible. Though dead he was not stiff, but moved when stirred. We then came to Haddenham and called on Mr Parrish, proprietor of the Green Dragon, and went with him and the constable to where the body lay, and found it in the same position. When I first returned to the cart, I saw nothing of the two people.

It had been between ten and eleven at night when Parrish was summoned. He saw the corpse and described it thus:

We found him lying on the road with his face down; his hat was over his eyes and bent a little. The collar which had been round the horse's neck was a small one, and could not have fallen off; it must have been taken off. When we examined the body we found it cold. I think it impossible the collar could be moved without help.

The corpse was taken to The Queen's Head pub in Haddenham. George Lever was one of the men who assisted in this task.

On Monday 27 October, the corpse was examined by two surgeons; Henry Reynolds of Thame, and Richard Lee of Haddenham. They surgically opened the skull and found the brain uninjured, and concluded that death was not caused by apoplexy. They then examined the ribs and found that five on the right-hand side had been damaged and fractured.

Richard Lee explained:

The first time I saw the deceased was about half past one on Sunday morning, having been called in by the constable's directions. I found, on my arrival, the extremities of the deceased quite cold and no sign of life remaining, except a slight degree of warmth about the chest. The only external unnatural appearance which I found was a slight abrasion on the right-hand side. On making a more minute examination of the body, I found that some of the ribs were fractured on the same side. I took the precaution of smelling the mouth of the deceased to ascertain, if possible, whether he was drunk at the time of death, and could not detect any smell of the sort. I think that I would have been able to discover some latent symptoms if he had been drinking to excess.

Reynolds gave more precise information after having examined the corpse in conjunction with his colleague:

> In the first instance, upon opening the skull, the first membrane was found perfectly healthy. In cases of blows on the head, this membrane seldom adheres. The membrane next to the brain, which in cases of apoplexy would be suffused, and which is in immediate contact with the brain, was more highly suffused with blood than in the natural state; but not more so than the circumstances which arose in the after examination would account for. There was no external bruises on the head, and on the body I found a slight bruise and abrasion of the skin, situated about an inch-and-a-half below the breast on the right side, which was the only exterior mark of injury on the whole body. On proceeding to strip off the integuments, I found five of the ribs fractured, the three lowest of which were broken in a second place, about an inch-and-a-half forwards, as if some extraneous body had beaten or forced in the whole piece; it must have been a tremendous blow, if it were a blow, which I cannot say. I found the right lobe of the liver ruptured to the extent of two inches or two-and-a-half inches into its absolute substance . . . the liver was diseased, but the disease was not one which would have killed the patient if he had not received external violence, it was what physicians call hydatids, which are generally enclosed in a capsule or sac; and the external violence having taken the direction of the sac, broke it. Without injury it might have remained to his death, without having burst.

The two surgeons determined that death would have occurred no later than ten minutes after Edden had been assaulted. He would not have been able to move by himself, let alone have risen, so could not have moved so far from the cart. Nor did they think that he could have been run over by a cart. A man could have committed the murder by stamping or kicking him. Some thought, though, that the death was accidental – that Edden had fallen from his cart whilst drunk, and then had been run over by another cart.

There were various footprints and some trouser prints at the scene of the murder. It was more than likely that these had been made by two different people as they were different sizes; nor could they have been made by people passing by along the road, because they had been made by people walking about. Whoever had killed Edden must have become fairly dirty. There were a few shillings in Edden's pockets, so the motive for the murder was not robbery. Samuel Taunton, a Bow Street Runner, was called upon as the principal investigating officer. He made enquiries at the various pubs along the route that the deceased man had taken.

The inquest began on 29 October at The Queen's Head pub in Haddenham. James Burnham was the coroner. Mr Rose, a juror, began by informing the coroner that the London newspapers were naming a man by the name of William Bailey, a horse dealer from Cuddington, as being the chief suspect, and was Burnham aware of this? Burnham was not, but said that such an insinuation was unjust.

Bailey had been at The Bottle and Glass pub at the hamlet of Gibraltar, further along the Oxford Road and about a mile from where Edden's corpse was found, on the Saturday night of the murder. He had been accused by Edden of being one of the men who had attacked him on the road four years ago. It was not known when Bailey returned home that night. Bailey was arrested the day after the murder. John Clisby of Thame, a publican, stated:

Mr Edden was stopped on the road from Aylesbury by persons who attempted to rob him. He came to his own house very dirty, and I washed his face. He went up to bed and I asked him who had made the attempt. He said one of them was a baker from Haddenham or Cuddington. Some time after that, William Bailey of Cuddington, passed by my house and the deceased said, 'That's the man who stopped me, and I would take my oath of it.' That was all that Edden then said to me. He had often told me that Bailey was one of the men who attempted

The Bottle and Glass pub, Gibraltar.

to rob him, and who said at the time, 'That's noble Edden of Thame.' I was at Cudidngton on last Sunday and saw this William Bailey and another man at the churchyard wall. I said to Bailey, 'What a serious thing it was that Edden was murdered, and he said in continuation that, 'There was no doubt those that stopped him last year upset him on this occasion.' He said they (himself, the deceased and others) were at the Rising Sun public house together and that he wanted to get him in his cart; but in consequence of it being loaded with coals, he could not give him a lift. At first he said that he had started for home before Mr Edden, and immediately afterwards he contradicted himself, and said that he had left Aylesbury an hour after him, and walked home with Mr Walker. There were other persons, named Reding, Munday and Crowdy, present, and we all noticed that at this time the countenance of Bailey very much changed when I put those questions to him.

In fact, Taunton was able to prove that Bailey could not have committed the crime, for he had been with Edward Walker, a respectable farmer of Chearsley, at the time of the murder. He said,

On Saturday last, I was at Aylesbury market and left it on foot at about six in the evening, in company with William Bailey, with whom I went to Cuddington. We called at The Bugle public house, where Bailey lighted his pipe. We stopped together at The Crown in Cuddington about half an hour till it was nearly nine o'clock. I left William Bailey and James Baker there together.

Bailey was cleared. Taunton added that he had found two witnesses from Aylesbury, who said that Edden had talked of possessing £20 that day, but Taunton did not believe that he had had that amount on him, as he was known to tell tales.

It was thought that several men might have been responsible for Edden's death. Sarah Salt had been leaving Haddenham in order to travel to Thame, and went by the turnpike road:

Three men overtook me about a mile from Haddenham, they said, 'Let us all keep together.' They asked me where I was going, having slacked their pace when they came up to me; I answered, 'To Thame,' and left the main road. I do not think I should know them if I were to see them. One of them was in a smock frock, he was stout, but not very tall, the other wore a hairy cap and dark clothes, the third did not come near me. I lost them near the hedge as I walked along towards Thame, as I walked on fast, fearful of them . . . I then lost the men altogether . . . The men came upon me very suddenly. I did not see them on the road before me as they came up.

Unfortunately, these men could not be traced; they had not subsequently called at any public house along the road. Sarah then said that she had seen, at about seven o'clock on Saturday night, two men she did not recognise going over a stile near Thame. They were going towards Aylesbury and walking very quickly. She thought they were tramps, but they did not carry sticks or bundles.

The motive for murder could well have been financial. Edden was thought to have possessed a considerable sum – £20 – on his person. He had been drinking in a number of pubs in Aylesbury and along the road. Others would have known that he had been speaking of his money. Yet two half crowns had been found in Edden's pocket, which indicated that robbery was not the motive. It was also recalled that Benjamin Collen had stolen eight sovereigns from Edden in August 1823 and had been subsequently hanged at Oxford. Perhaps the dead man's friends or family had decided to have their revenge on Edden?

Finally, it was time for the coroner, Burnham, to sum up. He complimented the jury on their patience, their intelligence and their resolve to see the inquiry concluded. After all, it had taken place over a number of days and this could have caused some of them great inconvenience. Since many of them had been making their own notes throughout, he said it was unnecessary for him to read over his own. The jury deliberated as to how Edden's death occurred and who was responsible for an hour-and-a-half, but could only conclude with the indefinite 'Murder against some person or persons unknown'.

The inquest was concluded on 10 November. It was uncertain whether one man or a group of men had killed Edden. It was also unclear as to why he had been killed, though robbery seemed a possibility. Could there have been a connection with the previous attack on Edden? The only suspect was Bailey, and he seemed to be in the clear as he lacked the opportunity to have committed the murder. The parish of Thame offered a reward of £50 for the identification of Edden's killer – the equivalent to the annual wage for many men.

Almost a year had passed before there was a major revelation in the case, and that was entirely due to the coincidence of two events. The first concerned a man who thought he was dying, and the second concerned his parents' illiteracy.

A Thame family, who kept a tripe shop in the town, received a letter from their son in London. Since neither could read, they passed the letter on to someone who could and they relayed the information that their son was in hospital. He believed that he was on his deathbed and requested that his parents visit him, to hear of his involvement in William Edden's murder.

Two constables of Thame, James Edden and Charles Seymour, were informed of this and were issued an arrest warrant on 11 August 1829. They went in search of the letter writer, one Solomon Sewell. He led the constables on quite a chase; Seymour recalled:

> As soon as he saw me in the field he ran away, and I followed him across the fields for two miles, over very thick hedges. He succeeded in escaping. I ultimately took him at his brother's. I said, 'Solomon, I've found you at last,' and he said, 'Yes, here I be.' The hedges he had gone through five days before had scratched him. He got through hedges so thick, I thought no man could get through.

Sewell was taken to Thame. At first he denied all knowledge of the crime, but eventually made a statement to William Ashurst, a magistrate, on 18 August:

> I am about 19 years of age. I have known Benjamin Tyler more than 12 months. I became acquainted with him by drinking at The Anchor and other public houses, where we met by chance. I do not ever remember meeting Edden on the Crendon road with Tyler. The death of Edden was at Michaelmass. There was not a charge of poaching against me at Thame Park. I only had written notice to keep off the ground. [I] Saw Tyler at between three and four o'clock in the afternoon of the death of Edden, but I did not speak to him. I was going fishing near Scotch-grove hill, and he overtook me between five and six o'clock. No other person was with him that I saw. It was dark. I did not speak to him. I had a net on my shoulder and a pole in my hand. Tyler told me he was going to kill Master Edden. I told him I would have no hand in it at all. He had a hammer in his hand, which was like a stone hammer. He had on a pair of green trousers and a long, green coat. I turned down to the river and threw my net once, before I went home. I saw no other cart but Edden's coming along the road. I was 20 yards from the cart. Tyler asked Edden for his money. Edden said he should not have it. I saw Edden strike him, and he fell back in the cart. I did not go near the cart myself; I heard someone say, 'Oh dear'. I ran home as fast as I could, round the back of Mr Hedges, and came into the road again at the turnpike. I did not see Tyler for a month afterwards. I never said anything to Tyler about the hammer. Tyler said he killed Lipscomb's pig with the same hammer – there were two, and he killed one. It was roasted at William

Furnall's. I did not have a bit of it. This was after Edden's death. I had no other conversation with Tyler then. It was the same hammer as killed master Edden. No one was with Tyler when he killed Edden. I saw Tyler at Sudbury, and Elizabeth Jones there too, and told her that if I was took up, Ben Tyler should not be five hours after me. Tyler said if I ever I said anything about Master Edden, he would blow my brains out; and if he did not kill me, his friends should.

This story turned out to be true, as Sewell mentioned that the hammer used to kill Edden was to be found in the cottage of Thame labourer, William Furnall, where it was later found. Sewell was committed to Aylesbury gaol, and a warrant went out for the arrest of Tyler. Oddly enough, on his way to the gaol, Sewell pointed out the spot where Edden was attacked.

John Birch, the constable at Hillingdon, soon arrested Tyler, who was in The Red Lion pub on the Uxbridge Road. Tyler told Birch, 'Very well, let me have my supper and I'll go with you. I know what you want me for, you want me for that job down in the country, that job of Edden's.' Tyler was brought before the magistrates, along with Sewell. Sewell looked very pale and depressed. He was dressed in a dirty duck smock frock and trousers of the same material. Tyler, on the other hand, seemed quite indifferent to the situation. He laughed several times during his examination, and seemed unaffected by the nature of the charge against him.

Tyler's lover, Ellen Hines – who he lived with – said that he could not have been involved in the murder, as he was with her on the night in question, except for a short amount of time, perhaps only half an hour. This was not enough time for Tyler to get to Haddenham and back, so therefore he could not have murdered Edden, as had been suggested. Tyler said he could bring additional witnesses to strengthen his case, but both prisoners were remanded in custody. Sewell stated that he had been with Tyler between five and six, as he was going fishing. Tyler then tried to prove his innocence by cross-examing his accuser, and asked Sewell where he was at the time of the alleged murder and he said he was at least a furlong away. Tyler retorted, 'What a rascal you must be to say that, Solomon. I am as innocent as an unborn babe.'

The investigation proceeded the next day, with the medical examination being recounted, followed by the constables' account of the arrests. Edden described the hammer he had found as:

A poleaxe. It was an instrument, which, if wielded by a strong arm, would inflict such a blow that it would put any man *hors de combat*. The handle was about two feet long; the iron, which it was fastened to, was about eight inches long, round at one end and sharp at the other; the sharp end was about two inches in length.

An interesting statement came from Mrs Edden. She said that in the spring of 1828 her husband had met Sewell and Tyler in his garden at Crendon. The two men were carrying something, but she did not know what it was. It was later learnt that Mr Harding had a sheep missing, and Mrs Edden believed that the bundle the two had been carrying was the stolen animal, as she had seen blood on their hands.

On the night of the murder, she was ironing and thought that she had heard her husband's voice, before seeing an apparition in his form. She then ran from the house and shouted, 'Oh dear God! My husband is murdered, and his ribs are broken.' Shortly after this, she asked Tyler to visit her house and stood him at the foot of her husband's open coffin. She asked him to touch the body but he refused to do so, muttering, 'Poor man, he has been murdered, safe enough.'

Sewell's mother, Charlotte, was next to give evidence and she spoke of her son's mental afflictions, stating that when he was born he was subject to fits within the year. I always gave him my own medicine. Since he has grown up he never was right; he could never learn his prayers, he could never count to 50, and never could lay money out.' However, others disagreed. An unnamed parish constable remarked, 'I have never heard that he has been subject to fits. I have known Sewell for sixteen or seventeen years. I think him capable of telling a story as it happens, and believe him to be in his right mind.'

The trial took place at the Spring Assizes at Aylesbury on Friday, 5 March 1830. It was attended by people of all ranks, anxious to hear the details of this strange case.

Mr Andrews, speaking for the Crown, gave the opening speech, providing a summary of the case against Tyler and Sewell. Firstly, evidence was given as to the finding of the corpse. Then there were several witnesses who gave statements about Sewell and Tyler. Francis Verry stated:

I know the man called Noble Edden. I know Tyler very well. On the Tuesday before Edden was found dead, I saw him and Tyler together at the Saracen's Head. They were having words. I heard Noble say to Tyler that, 'He [Tyler] was a sad rogue, and he knew enough to hang him, if he were to say all about him that he knowed'. Tyler made no reply that I heard. I went away and left them having words together.

This presented a motive for the murder; however, this was not proof in itself that Tyler had actually killed Edden – other witnesses provided this. John Foster, a resident of Thame, said:

> I know the two prisoners well. I recollect Edden's body being found; about a week or ten days before that I saw the prisoners together at the back of The Anchor by Lipscomb's, the butcher, between nine and ten at night. Tyler said to Sewell, 'It was done very easy,' to which Sewell made the answer, 'He would not do it; that would hang him,' and he repeated that it would hang him two or three times.

Ann Bonner was the next witness to give evidence. She recalled the following:

> Tyler was lodging at William Fernell's, a labouring man at Thame, when the body was found. I went to Tyler's house that evening and saw him. It was between five and six o'clock. I saw Tyler coming out of the house at first, speaking to Ellen Hines. I then saw Tyler put on a greatcoat of a dark colour. As he came out of the house. Hines said to him, 'How long shall you be gone?' He said, 'I don't know, according to what time I shall meet him' ... I saw him turn right to the Aylesbury road ... I saw him at ten o'clock the next morning at Fernell's, he was coming downstairs with a pair of high shoes in his hand; they were very dirty with road dirt. He then scraped both knees of his breeches; they too were very dirty with road dirt, of quite a light colour. I said to him, 'Old one, you got into the dirt last night?' He said, 'Yes, I did a bit.' I saw, under a deal table, a hammer all very dirty with road dirt.

Sewell and Tyler also made suspicious references to the murder afterwards. Matthew Townshend recalled seeing a group of men leaving a field a few days after the murder and Sewell said, 'I'll serve this here fellow the same as we served the old the other night.' William Hawes, who employed Sewell, talked about the murders and Sewell asked him, 'If you knowed, would you tell?' When Hawes replied positively, Sewell said, 'I'd be damned if I would, though.' Tyler had also avoided Edden's son, and when Tyler and his brother discussed the murder in the pub, on being overheard, they changed the subject.

Commenting on these statements, Sewell told the court, 'They are false, but I am willing to leave this world, and I will say it was false if it was the last breath I had to draw.' On another instance he said, 'I don't want to ask him nothing; he's come here to take a false oath, the same as Jem Edden: a damned rogue.' He made similar remarks throughout the case for the prosecution, even though the judge admonished him and recommended he be more guarded with his tongue. Tyler said nothing, but munched on bread and laughed.

The case for the prosecution ended with statements by the arresting constables and by the reading out of Sewell's confession. Ann Bonner identified the hammer as being the one she had seen at Tyler's lodgings.

The accused men were then asked if they had anything to say in their defence. Both stated their innocence. Tyler said, 'I am as innocent as a baby just born; I know nothing but what I have heard, just like other folk.' Sewell said, 'I'm innocent of the job; they told me what to say, and what they told me I said. It is all hearsay.' Tyler called on witnesses to testify in their favour, though his counsel advised against it. Their witnesses all attested that Tyler had worn a green jacket on the night of the murder, and the he had been seen at six, seven and ten o'clock. Ellen Hines had seen him at various times, but could not say specifically at what time.

The judge, Baron Vaughan, asked the prisoners if they had any other witnesses to call, and, learning this was not so, summed up the evidence. It took three hours in all, so great was the evidence that had been amassed. He said that Tyler was indicted as being the principal assailant as he had struck the first blow, but that Sewell had also been present when this had occurred and had assisted Tyler. He also drew the jury's attention to the points in their favour, and reminded them to give the accused men the benefit of any possible doubt. The jury only retired for ten minutes, and when they returned, the verdict they gave was guilty.

Tyler then asked to speak. Clasping his hands he said, 'May I burn forever and a day if I be'n't as innocent of this here as a baby.' Sewell made the same assertion and claimed that the verdict was 'all bribery that did it'. The judge then passed the death sentence on both men, and though the audience was universally affected, the condemned men seemed entirely unconcerned; Sewell smiled, and Tyler tottered from the court.

Neither man ever made a confession, and though Sewell appeared penitent on the scaffold, Tyler protested his innocence until his last breath. Both were hanged. The evidence against them was circumstantial and based, to an extent, on hearsay, but it was deemed good enough for the jury to decide on their verdict.

4

DREADFUL MURDER AT DORNEY

Dorney, 1853

One of the most barbarous murders to have been committed in Buckinghamshire took place within the household of Ralph William Goodwin, a bachelor gentleman and farmer of livestock at Burnham Abbey Farm, Dorney, where he had lived since 1850. He had been born in Datchet in about 1821 and lived with his widowed mother, Mary, until her death in around 1852. Three nights a week he slept at a neighbour's house. Mary Ann Sturgeon, aged thirty-six and from Suffolk, lived at the farm and was employed by Goodwin as his housekeeper. She had worked there for three months in 1853, having been previously employed by Miss Marsh at Britwell House, which was about a mile to the north within the same parish.

Another inhabitant at the farm was Moses Hatto, a groom. Hatto was in his twenties and had earned £5 for his previous year's work, and had been recently re-employed; now earning £8 per year. His duties included killing pigs, running errands and seeing to the horses. He was about 5ft tall and was described as a civil and obliging servant, who came across as being of good character. He had been born at Chilton in Berkshire to poor but honest parents; his father was an agricultural labourer. Hatto had earlier worked for Mr Plummer of Gray's, near Henley.

The farmhouse was a modern brick building and was located on the site of the ancient Abbey Farm, having been rebuilt for John Pocock (now deceased) some years previously. The builder had been one Mr H. Ingalton of Eton. The farm included other dwellings, notably a cottage occupied by John Bunce, the groundskeeper, in which lodged a number of labourers employed on the farm.

Burnham Abbey farmhouse.

On the fatal evening of Tuesday, 1 November 1853, Ralph Goodwin left home at six o'clock in order to visit a neighbour, not returning until half past eleven. Mary Ann, the housekeeper, called at John Bunce's house. She remained there until nine, before she returned to the farmhouse to prepare Moses Hatto's supper in the kitchen, which was separate from the rest of the house. Hatto slept in a chamber nearby, approached by a ladder from the kitchen.

Hatto had his supper and then went to bed. Later, he heard a noise from the kitchen which sounded like someone falling down, or so he thought at first. He went out to the farm cottage to find Bunce there. The latter was already partially dressed because he had needed to see to a colt in the yard. After this matter was attended to, the two men took a look around, but they could find nothing obviously wrong. Goodwin returned home at half past eleven, while Hatto saw to his horse as usual.

The master of the house let himself into the farmhouse using a latch-key, and was surprised to find the place in darkness. Lighting a candle, he was shocked to see, on the floor of the downstairs passageway, a human tooth and a hairpin. He then noticed a strong smell of burning and, upstairs, saw a dense cloud of smoke coming from Mary Ann's bedroom. He called her name, and, hearing no response, shouted for Bunce and Hatto to provide assistance. He then went into the housekeeper's room, where he was greeted with a horrifying sight.

The bedroom included a fireplace, which Goodwin, anticipating the arrival of relatives, had asked to be lit. Through the smoke, he could see Mary Ann's body. She was lying on the floor, her head near the mantelpiece and her legs on the hearthrug, in the direction of the bedstead. Flames were consuming her legs and the lower portion of her body. A dressing table and the linen in the room had been used as fuel, and the floorboards had burnt away so much that it was possible to see the floor joints. Delay in finding the fire could have resulted in the whole house being burned to the ground.

Once the flames had been extinguished, it was found that the head and upper part of the body, unaffected by the fire, had been savagely beaten, and that one tooth – found earlier by Goodwin – was missing. A large pool of blood had been formed near the head of the deceased and the sickening smell of roasted human flesh hung in the air.

The following day, John Charsley, the county coroner, held an inquest at Mile House on Colnbrook Road. Some thought that Hatto was responsible, but it soon transpired that he was innocent. Motive was discussed; at first robbery was excluded as a possibility, but Goodwin later reported that various valuable rings, a gold pencil case and other items of value were missing. It was also thought that the murder had taken place elsewhere and the corpse then moved to the bedroom, because one of Mary Ann's teeth had been found elsewhere in the house.

The inquest resumed the next day and the jury, respectable tradesmen of Burnham, were treated to additional evidence from the principal witnesses; the first of which was John Goodwin Ive of Langley Marsh, a farmer and also Goodwin's cousin, who Goodwin had visited on the night of the murder. He recalled that they had been together with Edward Peter Ive, John's brother, until a quarter to eleven, before Goodwin rode home. Ive stated that he did not know of any problems between the residents of Goodwin's household.

Goodwin himself then gave evidence. He stated that both the north and south doors were on the latch when he arrived home. He recalled that some time ago, Hatto had been asked by Mary Ann to lend him a sovereign, which Hatto had been initially reluctant to do so as he did not know how long he would be still be employed by Goodwin. However, the two servants usually got on amicably enough.

When Goodwin had arrived home, he had thought there was something unusual about Hatto's behaviour. Hatto asked him if anything was wrong and

Goodwin replied in the negative. Then Hatto went into the kitchen before he dealt with the horse, humming, both contrary to his usual behaviour. He then went to explain that, once alerted to the fire, he had called Bunce and Hatto to come with water and extinguish it. The labourers employed at the farm assisted too. Goodwin then expressed his shock at finding the body.

Mr Robarts, a surgeon from Burnham, had examined the body and reported his findings at the inquest. The back of the left hand was swollen and lacerated from blows caused by a blunt instrument. Some fingers were fractured, and it was presumed the unfortunate woman had raised her hand to vainly ward off the attack. There was evidence of several blows to the head and there were numerous wounds on the face. The legs had been burnt away. However, death had occurred before the body had been burnt, and elsewhere in the house, as bloodstains on the door and the floor of the corridor suggested that she had been dragged into the room. The imprint of a bloody hand had also been found on the passage wall.

John Bunce's wife, Jane, testified that she had heard the dogs barking at half past ten that night, but had thought it was some sparrow catchers entering the yard. She roused her husband just as Hatto called out, 'Bunce, get up, for I think there is someone about the place.' The two men investigated, and quieted the colts. Jane said that Mary Ann had visited her earlier that evening with a sticking plaster, as she (Jane) had hurt her finger. After helping her, Mary Ann had said, 'I must go into the house and get the boy's supper out.' She also said that she would then go to her room in order to avoid Hatto, as she found his conversation to be indifferent. The two had argued, but not on that day. Apparently, Hatto had heard a noise on the exterior door that evening, but did not mention it until after the murder had occurred.

It was later stated, though incorrectly, that Bunce threw gravel up to Mary Ann's window late that night. Hatto had asked him not to do it again as she would be asleep and it would only wake her. Bunce thought that he had seen a candle burning in the room. He knew very little of what happened in Goodwin's house itself.

Egglestone, a labourer employed on the farm, slept in the same room as Hatto that night, as he was anxious about sleeping alone. Hatto woke at four the next morning with a nosebleed, though Egglestone had never heard him complain of these previously. He had also noticed that during the fight against the flames, Hatto had slopped water against bloodstains near the door and had rubbed his hands against the marks.

Superintendent Symmington was in charge of the investigation. He had Hatto taken into custody, on the grounds that Hatto's trousers were marked with blood. There were bloodstains at the bottom of the bed in which he slept, but it was noted that these had been obliterated recently. There were also blood on Hatto's jacket, but, as he had helped to remove the body, it is possible that it could have been transferred at that time. It was also thought suspicious that Hatto had fallen into a pool of water shortly after the discovery of the body, for that would have given him the excuse to clean his clothing and try and remove any incriminating evidence. His trousers had been seen hanging in the kitchen on the Wednesday morning.

Further evidence had been found in a box belonging to Hatto, which contained various letters, one of which was addressed to Mary Ann's mother – others were addressed to Hatto's friends. Along with this, a bent poker was discovered in Hatto's bedroom – could this have been the murder weapon?

Hatto himself seemed unmoved. He had listened to the evidence carefully, but without emotion. In court he said, 'I can say nothing at all about the murder except that I myself am innocent of this crime. I have nothing further to say.'

At the summing up, the coroner suggested that it was possible that an outsider might have entered whilst Mary Ann was at the Bunces. He said that the evidence against Hatto was limited; though he was the last person known to have seen Mary Ann alive and that, as far as everyone was aware, they had been alone in the house at the time of the murder. Although his actions following the murder raised suspicion, there was no legal proof that Hatto had committed the crime. It seemed that Mary Ann had been attacked in her room, before running downstairs to sound the alarm – it was here, in the passageway on the ground floor where Goodwin had found the hairpin and tooth, that the murder took place. The jury discussed the case for an hour, but came to no conclusion and so the inquest was adjourned for another week.

In the interim, Superintendent Symmington made further investigations, chiefly aimed against Hatto. He tried to appear innocent, but the police thought that he was over-acting and became even more suspicious. He was kept in custody at the lock-up in Eton, but during his time there he did not mention the murder.

Mrs Bunce supplied them with fresh information about the deceased. Apparently, on the day before her death, Mary Ann had gone to Burnham village to post some letters. She had spent part of the journey in the company of John Marsh of Mills Farm at Brittle, with whom she used to work. The two enjoyed each other's company. Hatto had also been fond of Mary Ann, but his advances had been rebuffed. In fact, Mary Ann looked down on his lowly position, thinking herself above him. Hatto's jealousy had been apparent to all.

Burnham Abbey Farm entrance.

Goodwin also supplied the police with additional information. Apparently, Mary Ann would take the plates, which had been used that day and were stored in the sideboard drawer in the parlour, and lock them away upstairs before retiring for the night. On the night of the murder, not only had they not been moved – indicative of Mary Ann being prevented from doing so – but they had not been disturbed. This went against the theory of burglars being responsible for the murder.

The blood spots and stains were also examined afresh. The first traces were found in the doorway from the kitchen. Immediately above this doorway was Hatto's bedroom. Therefore, if Hatto had been in his room when the murder was being committed, which he claimed he had been, he could not have helped but hear the murder taking place, as well as the inevitable screams and cries for help that Mary Ann would have made when attacked. It was assumed that she had then tried to flee upstairs to her room.

Bunce gave further evidence against Hatto by casting doubt on the veracity of his earlier story. Hatto had claimed that he shouted for Bunce's help, but Bunce denied that he had done so. He said that the dog's barking and his wife's calls resulted in him looking out of the window to see what was amiss.

Seeing nothing, he dressed in order to go investigate, and it was only then that Hatto attracted his attention.

Inspector Langley, from London, came down to make further investigations. He found that between ten and eleven c'clock on the night of the murder, Hatto had visited Maidenhead railway station, about a mile or two from the crime scene. He used one of Goodwin's horses to ride there, allegedly for the purpose of enquiring if a parcel he was expecting had arrived. However, Langley wondered if Hatto had taken the opportunity to dispose of any incriminating evidence en route.

The inquest was resumed on Monday 8 November. Hatto was conveyed from Eton in a light chaise cart which travelled through Burnham, causing great interest among residents there. There was a strong local belief that he was guilty of the crime and concern that he might be lynched. When Hatto arrived at the inquest, he raised his chained hands in bravado to the court.

Goodwin was questioned by the coroner as to exactly what property had been stolen from his home. He ammended his earlier statement to say that these were two white-handled razors, a gold ring, two pencil cases, an ivory-handled knife with several blades, an ivory pocket table, two small keys and a button hook. He had realised three days after the murder that these had disappeared, but could not be sure that they had vanished on the night of the murder. He added that his housekeeper normally went to bed between nine and ten o'clock each night, and confirmed that Bunce and Hatto had removed her corpse from the room where she had been killed.

Surgeon Mr Robarts noted that Hatto had an extensive bruise on the right side of his forehead, as well as bruising on the knuckles of both his hands. Initially, these could have been mistaken for burns, but were now more noticeable as bruises. He then went on to say that he thought the deceased had been set on fire by a lighted candle, which had previously been in a candlestick in the room, and that it was likely she had been killed by blows from the poker found near her corpse.

After the evidence had been heard, Hatto was brought into the court, where he listened to the depositions made against him, before he was asked several questions. Firstly, he was asked whether he had anything to say, to which he replied, 'I did not tell the carter that I was coming here for a parcel on Thursday night.'

After ten minutes of discussion, the jury concluded that Hatto was guilty of wilful murder. The coroner ruled that he should be held in custody at Aylesbury until the assizes of the following year. He was conveyed there under the escort of Superintendents Symmington and Superintendent Thomas.

The trial began at the Spring Assizes at Aylesbury on 8 March 1854. Lord Campbell presided as judge, while Mr Edward Power spoke for the prosecution and Mr J.B. Parry acted at Hatto's defence counsel. Although Hatto was poor and friendless, local noblemen and gentry contributed towards the expense of a proper defence for him. Lord Carrington and Baron Rothschild each gave ten guineas, and the Society for the Prevention of Capital Punishment also gave financial assistance.

Although the majority of witnesses had already given their evidence, Daniel Besley, a coachbuilder of Abingdon, was examined by Mr Power. He had once employed Hatto, and in October 1853 Hatto had visited him at his home. Besley had asked him, 'Well, William, how are you getting on?' Hatto merely replied, 'Tolerably,' and Besley made another enquiry, 'Have you left, or are you going to leave?' Hatto said, 'I don't know. I like my master very well, but the servant and I can't agree very well.' Clearly the seeds of Hatto's discontent had been laid some time before the murder.

Superintendent Symmington was questioned about the time that Hatto was in his custody. He told the court that Hatto had told him the following: 'The people think more about it than me. I don't fret; it's no use, what's done can't be helped. I suppose they'll do what they like with me. They said I took a handkerchief and keys from the deceased'.

Samuel Perkins, Superintendent at Eton, recalled talking to Hatto. He stated his innocence and that he had not seen Mary Ann after she had given him his supper, he then added, 'Oh yes, she came into the kitchen again and asked if I had sufficient.' The case for the prosecution was then concluded.

Hatto did not seem to take the trial very seriously. He smiled throughout and nearly laughed at one stage. On the second day, after being advised by his solicitor, he adopted a more serious attitude.

The trial recommenced the following day. The coroner's clerk, Robert Eckford, read out Hatto's deposition. It ran as follows:

I live with Mr Goodwin in the capacity of groom. Mr Goodwin left the house at 6 and returned a little after eleven last evening. I was in the kitchen when he returned. I had my supper between eight and nine. The deceased was there for part of the time. She went into the house. I went to bed as soon as I had finished my supper. About a quarter before eleven I heard a rumbling noise like a rumbling against the door. I then lay down and about a quarter of an hour afterwards I heard the dogs barking. I got up and called to Bunce, the foreman, and he got up. There were some colts loose in the yard. We walked round the premises, but could not see or hear anyone. I then went and tried the passage door near to the kitchen, and it was fastened, and there I remained till Mr Goodwin came in. He came in shortly afterwards. I told him, as the dogs had been barking, we went to see whether anyone was about in the premises. Mr Goodwin went in at the door in the north front. I don't know of any door being unfastened. I used to have words with the deceased because she wished me to do more work than I thought I could do. I got wet in going around the yard and changed my clothes. After Mr Goodwin came home I assisted in taking water upstairs to put the fire out, which was raging in the maidservant's room. I then saw Mary's body with the legs on fire, and blood against the door. I threw gravel up at the window of the deceased's before Mr Goodwin came home, but I could not hear her. I don't know anything of the poker produced. There was a light in the deceased's room. The blind of the window was down. I don't know if she had any followers.

Mr J.B. Parry then addressed the jury on the prisoner's behalf. He claimed that the introduction to the case had been unduly harsh against the prisoner. He also stated that the whole case for the prosecution rested on the assumption that Mary Ann must have screamed when attacked and that Hatto must have heard it. A recent experiment at the farmhouse conducted by the prosecution to show that Hatto would have heard the screams from his room was condemned as being unusual and a false device designed to give the jury the impression that Hatto was guilty. Parry went on to claim that most of the witnesses only offered circumstantial evidence. The lack of a motive was also commented upon. Finally, he appealed to the jury that the case against Hatto was based on suspicion only and that, as his life was at stake, the jury should give him the benefit of the doubt and be guided by God towards mercy. This address lasted three hours, and afterwards the jury were allowed a quarter of an hour's break before the judge gave the summing up. He recounted the entire case for them and urged them to come to the correct decision by careful and calm reflection of the evidence laid before them.

The jury retired at 2.20 p.m. and did not return until 5.40 p.m. – a lengthy time indeed. The verdict they delivered was guilty. The judge passed the death sentence. Hatto heard this with stolid indifference. He was asked to make his peace with God, and Hatto replied, 'Thank you my Lord,' and bowed respectfully to the judge. The court broke up at six o'clock, and within half an hour news of the verdict had spread through the town; furthermore, that Hatto had subsequently confessed all.

Indeed he had, though a little later than was first reported. After the verdict had been pronounced, Hatto expressed a desire to make a full confession before the prison chaplain, Revd G.A. Cuxson, and James Sheriff, the governor. The following is the written confession:

Bucks County Prison, Aylesbury

March 9th, 1854, 8 p.m.

Moses Hatto, in the presence of the governor and the chaplain, says that, for the relief of his own conscience, and in order that what he is about to state may prove a warning to others not to be listeners, he desires to make this following confession to go forth to the public: 'The first beginning of it was on the Wednesday before Old Michaelmass day last, when Mary Ann Sturgeon asked me to lend her a sovereign to send home to her friends. This was said in the kitchen, in the presence, but not in the hearing of, Mr Willis' cook from Norfolk, and it was plain that Sturgeon wished to leave the money without the knowledge of Mr Willis' cook. They were both of them dressed, and just starting to drink tea at Burnham. I went upstairs and fetched my money, amounting to about a guinea. I asked her when she thought she would be able to return it again, as I was going to leave. I told her that I had lent money before, and that I could never get it back again. She said that she had been served the same. She said she had never been so insulted in her life as she felt to be by that question, adding that she could easily send it to me, wherever I might be, by post, at the same time she turned herself from me, saying, 'I will never speak a good word of you again.' On the following Sunday week, in the afternoon, I was accompanying her, as usual, part of the way towards Burnham Church, when I told her I would lend her either one or two sovereigns if she liked. She made little or no reply, but in the course of the week she twitted men several times with my having refused her. I begged her not to tell me of it again, promising to treat her with half a crown's worth of anything if she would not do so. She replied that she would not tell me of it again, but repeated that she would never speak a good word of me. On Monday October 31, as we sat together at dinner, she began twitting me and all the farm labourers, the master as well, with being a shabby lad, saying that she had heard the character of Burnham Abbey before she ever came there. I said, 'I know where you got all that from, two women have been telling you that.' She denied it. I persisted that I knew. She got up from the dinner, shook her head at me, and said, 'I meant to have told you, but I won't and you shall never know.' The rest of that evening she would not speak to me, nor sit with me, but went upstairs. All that afternoon she was very angry with me. The next day it was worse. I was employed that day in cleaning the tin, silver and copper ware, and other indoor work. When I asked her for anything, she said I might get it from where I liked, or do what I liked, for she would not speak to me again. That evening she would

Burnham parish church.

not speak to me, nor sit with me. She set my supper out, and afterwards went to Bunce's and I went to my stable. Some time afterwards I suspected that something wrong was going on about me between her and the Bunces, at Bunce's house, so I went, with my shoes in my hand and listened at Bunce's door, which was about a foot open. I heard them talking about me, and then Bunce said, 'He's a very big eater, isn't he?'

'Yes,' said she, 'he's a very big eater.'

'Well,' said Bunce, 'Mrs Finch said he was a very big eater, but he did not eat much bread, but I thought she was joking.'

Sturgeon said, 'He's not a big bread eater, but he eats so much meat.'

Mrs Bunce said, 'I am glad that he has got his master.'

'Leave him alone,' said Sturgeon, 'he's hanging himself every day. He'll soon do it. Leave him alone.' That throwed me at once. I was drove into an agony with it. To think that I had been working for her, neglecting my own work all day! How often had I favoured her and denied myself, and stayed at home while she went out, and now for me to hear all this! It drove vengeance upon me to hear her running me down to all eternity. They were then about parting, so I leaped over the palings, went into the stable, finished my work, and went indoors for my supper. Then, to throw more madness upon me, instead of bringing me a pint of beer as usual, she brought me the pint half full. I could not eat my supper, but drank my beer and she asked if I had had sufficient. I said, 'I have had sufficient.' These were the last words I ever spoke to her. She looked so evil at me, and I was so thrown that I hardly knew – indeed, I did not know – where I was, or what I had done. I stood with my hand clenched, ready to strike her; but I could not. Then she went into the larder. I then took the iron lard beater and stood at the door, thinking to strike her down as she returned, but I could not do it, and thinking to drive it out of my mind, I went out of doors. I wished I might hear my master returning home. Then I went in again. She again went into the lard house. I again took up the lard beater, and, on her return, I knocked her down in the passage. As she was very strong, she threw me over once, but she was no more than a child to me. She said, 'Don't, my good fellow.' I accidentally dropped the lard beater. I kicked her with vengeance. She screamed very loudly. We had a great struggle in the passage. I kicked her two or three times. It was in the dark, for her candle had fallen and the light had been put out. I left her where the grease and blood and tooth and hairpin were found, and I returned into the kitchen, I think to fetch a light. She got up and ran upstairs. I followed her and caught her at her bedroom door and I threw her up in the passage. She screamed again. I kicked her two or three times. She cried, 'Lord, have mercy upon my soul.' I caught hold of her and pulled her into the bedroom, struck her on the head with the poker two or three times, and broke the poker. I pushed her clothes against the grate, and they caught fire. I left her room. Then I went to my own bedroom and changed my trousers, shirt and stockings because they were bloody. I went back to her bedroom and looked how the body was going on, and I took down a dress that was hanging on a peg, and threw it over her. Then I went to Mr Goodwin's room to take away something, to make believe that some thief had been in the house. I wiped the lard beater on a dishcloth, and I burnt the bloody string on which it usually hung. Then I cut my bloody shoes to pieces with one of Mr Goodwin's razors. Then I bolted the passage door inside, and went out by the south front door. Then I went and hid, among the shrubs, the pieces of my shoes. I also hid the articles stolen from Mr Goodwin's room under the trees in the meadow. They are still under the tree – between the tree and the ditch. The tree is a withy pollard, about the second or third near the Cippenham footpath. I have never seen the latter since, but the former I removed from the scrubs the next morning, and threw the soles into a shallow well in the meadow, by the garden gate, and the upper leathers into the drain leading to it. They are there now.

After I had hidden the pieces of shoes in the scrubs, I went and hid my shirt in the pond close to the house, treading it into the mud, and my trousers under the roof of the coal pen. Then I went and lay down. Then the dogs began to bark. I called Bunce from my window. Mr Goodwin returned home. After six o'clock on the Wednesday morning I went and removed my shirt from the pond, and my trousers from under the roof of the coal pen, and I hid them in the ditch near the meadow. The drawers, which I wore at the time of the murder, were bloody at the right knee, but it escaped the notice of the constable, because the drawers fell down in a wrinkle when I was stripped. It was Symmington who first gave me in charge to Webb.

When I first struck Sturgeon it must have been between nine and half past nine o'clock. I did not break up the deal table in Sturgeon's bedroom, but it caught fire and was burnt in two, and fell upon her. I never placed any napkins or anything else under her. They might have fallen on the floor off the dressing table. I think that if Bunce or any good strong man had come in when she was screaming, I should have attacked him. I thought of that at the time. Some time in the last fortnight of October, Sturgeon threatened to stab me if I ever mentioned a word about her, even half a sentence, either to my master or to any one else. I said, 'But O! I would get out of your wa.' She replied, 'It would be of no use, I should meet with you sometime, and would do it.' Perhaps I might have thrown two dresses instead of one upon her, but after the fire had burnt through the floor, it seemed to burn with a draught. I consider it my duty to uncover my sin. I do not hope for any gain in this world, but I hope for one in the next.

It was believed that this was a genuine confession, for his subsequent conduct was good and he appeared to pay attention to the chaplain's ministrations. Yet there were some factual discrepancies. Although the clothing and other incriminating evidence were found where he claimed they were, the items stolen from his master were not in the location stated. It was also thought that he had added material to help the fire burn and had used oil or naphtha to make the body flammable.

The Society for the Prevention of Capital Punishment, who had helped fund Hatto's defence, did not take the judge's sentence as final. They canvassed for a petition, asking that the sentence be commuted to one of imprisonment. It was sent to Lord Palmerstone, the Home Secretary. However, the politician stated that, 'The law must take its course.'

Moses Hatto was executed in front of the county gaol at Aylesbury on the morning of 24 March 1854. This was the first execution that had taken place before the new prison. The scaffold was erected over the entrance gateway, near to the houses of the chaplain and the governor. When Hatto was led to the gallows, he appeared depressed, but walked without assistance. The crowd that gathered to watch was small in number and there was little excitement; there was no hooting or shouting. Even so, thirty constables were present to deter any pickpockets. The hangman quickly performed his duties and Hatto died after a few brief struggles.

What should we make of this crime? It seems that the grudge between Hatto and Mary Ann developed from both sides. Hatto seems to have been very much attached to her and this was unwelcome to her, as she was seeing another man. Her manner of dealing with this unwelcome attention was not very tactful and resulted in turning Hatto's love to hate.

5

MASSACRE AT DENHAM

Before Denham became better known for being the setting for two of the more popular screen representations of crime fiction, it was where the county's worst single crime took place. In the 1960s, it provided the backcloth for the opening sequences to the Margaret Rutherford *Miss Marple* comedy mysteries. Forty years later, the church provided the setting in an episode of *Midsomer Murders*. Yet there is nothing remotely entertaining about the murders committed there which shocked the country in 1870.

Emanuel Marshall was born in 1836 in Hillingdon, Middlesex, to William, a labourer, and his wife, Mary. He was baptised at St Laurence's Church, Cowley on 3 April of that year. His family moved to Denham shortly afterwards. There were four children, with Emanuel being the youngest (his two brothers had emmigrated to Australia by 1870). As an adult, Marshall was employed in a shop in Denham. He married Charlotte, four years his junior, in Stow, Suffolk, in 1860. A year later he, Charlotte and his widowed mother were living together in Denham, and he was working as an engine fitter. Over the next few years, the couple had four children; Mary, born in 1862, Thirza in 1864, Gertrude in 1866, and Francis William in 1869. By 1870, Marshall was a blacksmith, and was respected by his neighbours as hardworking and sober. His sister, Mary Ann, who had left Denham in the 1850s, had returned to the family home. She was due to marry George Amor of Hertfordshire at the parish church of St Mary's on Wednesday 24 May. This led to young Francis having to stay a few days with an aunt in nearby Uxbridge, due to lack of room in their cottage. The

Denham village.

family had attended the market in Uxbridge on Saturday 20 May, whilst two of the girls were seen playing in the road.

On Monday 22 May, a shocking discovery was made, though accounts vary as to how this occurred. One has it that a wedding dress was being delivered to the house, another that two labourers called at the cottage needing Marshall to undertake some work for them, and yet another states that Marshall's sister-in-law went to the house for afternoon tea. Finding the place locked up and not hearing anything, she became worried and asked two men to help open it. PC Charles Taverner, who was based in Denham, was summoned to the cottage. He later informed the magistrates at the inquest of the following events:

> I went to the house and found the doors open. I found two bodies – the wife and the sister – lying just inside the door and the sister's feet towards her head. A petticoat covered them. About two feet from them was a sledgehammer . . . this was covered with blood. I then went into the wash house and found the bodies of the three children. I found an axe . . . also covered with blood. There were extensive wounds on the heads of all of the bodies . . . I found the body of Emanuel, the father, in the forge, lying flat on his face, with his hands stretched out.

The entire family had been massacred in a few moments of horror and savagery. All the corpses were dressed in their night attire except Marshall, who had his work clothes on, though not his boots. A sack had also been found over his head. A poker was found near the bodies, and it too had been used as the murder weapon, along with the axe and sledgehammer.

Upstairs, all three of the beds had been slept in, and Taverner could find no evidence of any struggle having occurred. He thought that they must have hurriedly left their beds and run downstairs. Another set of clothes was also found in the cottage, and Taverner described these thus: 'There is blood on these clothes. There was a pair of boots, trousers, a coat, and a cord jacket. A cord vest, a slop, a deer stalker's hat, and a red and white common plaid neck cloth.'

Taverner had seen a man wearing these clothes on the previous morning. He had been on patrol and saw a man who was dressed as a shabby mechanic. The man told the constable that he had seen a man threatening to throw his wife into the nearby canal. He went onto explain that he was a stranger in these parts and asked for directions to the Marshall's home, which, presumably, he was given before he headed off in that direction, leaving Taverner to continue his beat.

There were additional witnesses who saw this mysterious man. However, Elizabeth Simpson, who saw him at seven o'clock that Sunday morning, thought the man was Marshall himself, as he was dressed in Marshall's clothes and was coming from the direction of Marshall's home. He was also carrying a carpetbag (none such had been seen by Taverner a few hours previously). Elizabeth was looking for a lost key and she walked with the man for a while. He told her the same story as he had told the police officer. When she mentioned to him that she had mistaken him for the blacksmith, he replied that the family had left their cottage earlier that morning and had gone on holiday.

Another Denham resident who met the man that morning was John Smith, a coal dealer. He was sitting outside his cottage just before eight o'clock. The man offered to sell Smith a watch, but he declined as he already possessed one. However, when the stranger offered to buy Smith a pint of beer in an Uxbridge pub, he consented readily.

This pub may have been The Dog and Duck, for at about eight o'clock, Sarah Alderman, the publican there, was asked to serve drinks. She initially refused because she could not sell drinks until 12.30. The man retorted that he had travelled from High Wycombe and so claimed traveller's rights to hospitality. Sarah took his shilling and provided him with beer. As with Elizabeth, she thought that the clothing he was wearing was similar to Marshall's and she also noticed the carpetbag. The customer seemed tired, but only stayed for ten minutes and did not even finish his drink.

Superintendent Thomas Dunham of the Buckinghamshire Constabulary, and based at Slough, arrived later that evening to take charge of the investigation. He noted that Charlotte and her sister-in-law had their nightdresses torn and that the latter was wearing boots. It appeared that they had been killed before being dragged to where they were found, and this movement had led to their clothing being torn. The elder children's corpses were in the kitchen and the younger one was found next to her grandmother, dressed in only a chemise. Marshall appeared to have been dragged around the forge, judging by his appearance, for his face was as black as coal because of the ash on the floor. Upstairs, two drawers of a bureau had been opened and a watch case was found to be empty.

An initial theory was that Marshall, suffering from homicidal mania, had killed his family and had then committed suicide. Yet it was quickly found that this was impossible, for the wounds on his person could not have been committed by him; nor were the weapons near to his corpse, nor could he have put a sack over his own head.

Another theory was that this was a revenge attack on Marshall. In December 1869, he had witnessed arsonists setting fire to Ivy House, just to the south of Denham on the main road to Uxbridge. He later testified against two men in court. Before they were sent to gaol for a few months, they swore revenge against him. Could this have been their work? Or was robbery the motive? However, some of the victims still had rings on their fingers, making robbery seem an unlikely motive.

In High Wycombe, a young man called Robinson was in a pub, discussing the murders. He described the position of the victims. Suspicion fell on him and he was taken before the magistrates. They remanded him in custody, though not for long.

It seemed that the case would be a difficult one. The killer had escaped on the Sunday morning and there was no clue to his identity, or to the motive. With nothing in the way of forensics, fingerprinting or any other scientific aids, matters did not look good for the police.

The following day, a major manhunt was initiated. Enquiries were made by Detective Superintendent Williamson and Inspector Sutton in Uxbridge. Every alehouse and lodging house in the vicinity of the two major towns of Uxbridge and Brentford was visited. But there was no need for all this, for the police had a lucky break in finding Charles Coombes, who had a story to tell. He was an Uxbridge bricklayer who resided at Mrs Ballam's lodging house. On the Monday evening he had been in the Queen's Head pub in Uxbridge when he heard about

The Queen's Head pub, Uxbridge.

the murders. He was with another man with whom he shared a lodging house, who asked Coombes to show him out of the pub by the back door. After having done so, Coombes returned to the pub to hear the rest of the shocking news. His friend returned ten minutes later. Coombes had an early night for he needed to be at work by six o'clock the next morning. On the previous day, Coombes had been offered a silver watch by his new acquaintance, which he declined, so it was pawned instead. Flush with money, the man treated both Coombes and two women to drinks on both Sunday and Monday evening.

On Tuesday morning Coombes began to entertain suspicions about the man, and told his employer about this. He then reported the matter to the police. The desk sergeant at Uxbridge then showed Coombes the clothes that had been found at the Marshalls', which evidently did not belong to any of the deceased. Coombes then told the desk Sergeant that he had seen these being worn by his friend on the day that he had first met him, which was on Saturday 20 May. He knew this man as Jack, but his real name seems to have been John Owen, though he went by a number of aliases. He had been in prison earlier that year for theft and had recently been released.

On that Saturday, Coombes recalled that Owen had no money and lacked a carpetbag. He had also declined Coombes' offer of a visit to a pub, but instead left the lodging house which he was sharing with Coombes and went out that night, not returning until about ten o'clock on Sunday morning. According to Coombes, 'He was then attired quite differently from what he had on when he first took the lodgings.' Coombes told Owen, 'Why, I don't know you again, hardly.' Owen explained that he had visited his brother's house and the latter had supplied him with a new set of clothes. When the landlady heard of this, she was puzzled, remarking, 'There is something done wrong by that fellow, for it don't stand to reason that a brother would strip himself of clothes and a watch.'

Coombes then explained that Owen told him that he was going to Reading. At about five on Tuesday morning, he came into Coombes' bedroom and asked, 'Have you any tobacco?' Coombes had not, and then was asked if he had any breakfast going spare. Coombes said he would happily share what little he had. Owen then made a fatal mistake. He told Coombes he planned to take the six forty-five train to Reading. At this time there was a branch line from Uxbridge which ran south to West Drayton station, and from there a train could be taken to Reading.

That same afternoon, Coombes went to Reading by train. Superintendent Dunham had returned to Slough already and there he met Coombes. The two travelled on to Reading and met PC Toulman in the Berkshire town. They searched numerous lodging houses until they reached the Oxford Arms, on Silver Street. Dunham later recalled, 'I went into the kitchen, which was behind the house, and there were about a dozen men and women there. Coombes at once pointed out Owen.' After being recognised, Owen said, 'I never murdered man, woman, or child,' though he was later to deny having said these words. According to Dunham:

> I crossed over to him at once and seized him by the throat. The Reading policeman who was with me – Toulman is his name – said, 'Mind, he's pulling something out of his pocket!' and, crossing over, I seized his arm, and took hold of the pistol which the prisoner had taken from his pocket.

The gun had been loaded up to the muzzle with powder, slugs and pieces of iron wire. Dunham remarked, 'You are charged with murdering seven people, among them Emanuel Marshall,' before handcuffing him. Owen replied, 'I have not murdered anyone but I know who did.' Dunham said, 'You have the murdered man's boots and some of his clothes on.' Owen answered, 'That may be.' He was then searched. Among his possessions was an Uxbridge pawnbroker's ticket for a silver watch with a gold chain that was missing from the Marshalls' home. There was other evidence that he had pawned the dead man's waistcoat and coat at a pawnbroker's in Union Street, Reading, for four shillings. Five shillings and sixpence were the only coins found on his person. The pawnbrokers in both Reading and Uxbridge identified Owen as the man who had done business with them so recently. Later, the clothes found at the Marshall house were recognised by Thomas Paulton, a warder at the Clerkenwell House of Correction – which Owen had so recently quitted – as belonging to Owen.

Owen was then escorted to Reading police station, and was then taken to Slough by train that evening. Mr Boyce, the governor of Reading Gaol, identified Owen as a former inmate, who had stolen a barrow from Reading cemetery about eight or nine years ago. More recently, he had been convicted of stealing a lamb in Abingdon, and had been released from Reading Gaol on 8 January 1870. He had then been known as John Jones, and had told his warder that he would never enter Reading Gaol ever again.

Superintendent Dunham was joined by the county's Chief Constable, Captain John Tyrwhitt Drake, a former soldier, and they escorted Owen from the gaol to the railway station. Watching them was a crowd of at least 1,000 people, who bore Owen much ill will, though it was only expressed by their hissing at him. Prisoner and escorts left for Slough on the ten past eight train.

On the following day, Wednesday 24 May, Owen was brought before the magistrates at the Sessions House at Slough police station. It was learnt that he also went under the aliases John Jones and John Jennings. It was uncertain whether he was married or a widower, or whether he had once been a Birmingham blacksmith or a Staffordshire boilermaker. What was certain was that he had a long criminal career behind him, chiefly for theft in and around London. He was also something of a figure of interest to the crowd who wanted to catch a glimpse of him. 'The man, seen anywhere and under any circumstances, would be judged to be a particularly brutal type, his head indicating a thoroughly animal organisation. As seen in the dock, the peculiarly unprepossessing characteristics of the man, were, perhaps, heightened by the circumstances which surrounded him.' Although Owen tried to appear cool, when he was shown the clothes that he had worn when committing the murders, which were still bloodstained, the colour drained from his face.

Superintendent Dunham presented his evidence to the magistrates about his examination of the scene of the crime on the Monday evening. Coombes then gave evidence:

I can swear to the cap (which is a peculiar one) and to the corduroy jacket. I should not like to swear to the boots. The prisoner wore that cap, which I noticed particularly, as it had a narrow brim, and the jacket on Saturday.

There was some difference of opinion between Coombes and Owen over when they first met on that day, with Coombes alleging it was three o'clock and Owen saying it was two hours later. Coombes admitted he was not certain when the meeting occurred.

Owen was to be remanded in custody for another week. The prisoner was taken to Aylesbury prison by train.

The police theorised that Owen had arrived at the Marshalls' house when all were asleep. He woke Marshall up, by breaking into the smithy to look for weapons. When Marshall hastily dressed and went to the smithy, he was killed by the intruder. His wife then went downstairs to see what had happened to her husband and she too met her fate. The rest of the family were then despatched as they ventured downstairs. The cottage was then plundered of its valuables. It was believed that Marshall was in debt to Owen and was killed because he refused to pay up.

On 26 May, the funeral service for the family was held at St Mary's Church in Denham. All of the family were laid to rest there, except Marshall's mother, who was buried at Hillingdon. A large stone marks their resting place. The cruel irony of the burial was that it was on the same day that Mary Marshall was to have been married at the same church. Indeed, the vicar, Revd Charles Joyce, recalled that only the previous Sunday he had been reading the banns of marriage for the third and final time – at the same time that the bride-to-be was lying murdered in the cottage nearby. During the sermon, scarcely a dry eye could be seen, everyone present being deeply overcome by the excellent sermon delivered.

The inquest re-commenced on 27 May. Superintendent Dunham gave his evidence, to be followed by Dr John Ferris of Uxbridge. He had been present on the evening of the discovery, and was now assisted by three other doctors. According to him, the murder had occurred at about three o'clock on Sunday morning. He then went into detail about each corpse. It does not make for pleasant reading. After noting some grazes on Marshall's fingers, suggesting that he had tried to defend himself, Dr Ferris said:

There were four wounds on the face, one over the right eye, one over the nose, one over the left eye and a deep one on the chin. The upper and lower jaws, even to the bone under the eye, were completely smashed in. On the head, the hair was matted

St Mary's Church, Denham.

with blood, and ashes were on it, and on the scalp were five wounds, one on the left side of the head, one behind it, an inch and a half long, another small one behind that, on the back of his head, a large one, on the right side a long lacerated wound. The skull was not fractured by one of these. There was a fracture on the base of the skull from right to left, to such an extent that the skull could be pulled in half. The scalp wounds were probably produced by a poker, and the smashing of the face and fractures by a sledgehammer, or the back of an axe.

The description of the wounds suffered by the rest of the family was equally distressing. Ferris then spoke of the six-year-old girl, Thirza:

On her there was no fracture or bruise on limbs or body, but there was a wound on the scalp and protrusion of brain, and blood was oozing from the right ear, behind which was a small cut. The face was uninjured. On removing the scalp an open face to the brain, of five inches by four inches, was disclosed – in fact, the whole right side of the skull was smashed, to the right side of the spine. The injuries on the child were produced by one blow of the sledgehammer.

Ferris then discussed eight-year-old Mary's wounds:

[She] had no bruise or fracture on body or limbs, but on the head was a semi-circular wound five inches in length, which almost completely cut off the right ear, a small wound above the right ear, other wounds on the back of the head, and near them a 'starred' cut. Three of these were made by a poker, but the 'starred' cut could not have been produced by any instrument yet found. There was a wound on the right side of the face, and both jaws were broken. Inside the skull there was a puncture wound corresponding with the 'starred' cut on the outside, and the base of the skull was fractured across, dividing the skull in half.

Next, the wounds of four-year-old Gertrude were described:

[She] had blood coming from nose, mouth, and ears, but she had no injuries whatsoever to body or limbs. All the bones on the left side of the head were completely smashed in – the temple bone alone being intact. Many fragments of bone were detached and there was much blood on the brain. All the injuries to the body were probably done by a sledge hammer.

Mary Ann Marshall's injuries were the next to be described:

No injury was on the body or limbs. There was a slight cut on the upper lip, a wound an inch in length outside the left eye, the teeth of the upper jaw were knocked into her mouth, a wound an inch-and-a-quarter long was down the parting of the hair, a wound three inches long was on the right side of the head, and these appeared as if done by a sharp axe. There was a large quantity of blood between the brain and the skull, and inside a large amount of blood again, and a fracture at the base so great that the skull could be pulled in half. Several pieces of bone were detached.

Finally, there Charlotte, Marshall's wife:

No injuries were done to the body or limbs. On the face the left eyelid was bruised, and there was blood oozing from the left ear. There was a jagged transverse wound an inch long over the right ear, a wound three inches long at the back of the head, much blood under the scalp, and a fracture at the base of the skull right across, so the skull could be pulled in half. The injuries were done by a sledgehammer or the back of an axe.

Ferris' professional fellows said that they concurred with him in his assessment of the wounds and how they had been caused.

Mary Sparks, Marshall's sister-in-law, identified Owen's costume as one that her late brother-in-law once owned. Later, a key found at Owen's lodging house was found to fit the lock of Marshall's house. The inquest concluded that this was a case of murder and that Owen was responsible. He was ordered to stand trial at the county assizes at Aylesbury in July.

Interest in the murders among the public was very great indeed. Not content with reading the newspaper accounts, some made pilgrimages to the murder site. Although the cottage was guarded by the police, people travelled from London and elsewhere to Denham by train and horse power. They wanted to gape at the house and some had hoped to take souvenirs back with them. Such behaviour was not uncommon in cases of murder both then and now, especially if they are particularly gruesome or include numerous victims.

Owen was examined by the magistrates one final time before being sent to trial, and this led to additional information being given about the man's movements prior to his meeting Coombes in Uxbridge. Owen was released from Coldbath Fields prison in south London on the Saturday at nine o' clock (he had been imprisoned there two months previously, for stealing shirts in Uxbridge). He had tramped westwards along the Uxbridge Road. At Hanwell Bridge he met Henry Salter, a carter, who was returning to his employer, an Uxbridge miller. Owen asked if he could have a lift in the cart and Salter obliged. Owen told the man that he was penniless, but that he had a brother in Uxbridge who would

Hanwell Bridge. (Courtesy of Paul Lang)

assist him. He alighted at the Green Man pub at 5.30 p.m. Salter identified the clothing found at Marshall's house as those he had seen Owen wearing on that day. It was also ascertained that the pistol in Owen's possession in Reading had once belonged to Marshall, and that it had been charged by an Uxbridge blacksmith on the day following the murders.

The trial commenced at Aylesbury on 21 July, before Judge Baron Channell. He addressed the jury thus, 'This is one crime of great magnitude which will require your attention, but which I think will not make any considerable demand on your time.' He then gave a summary of the case. Yet the trial proper did not begin until the following day, with one Dr John Thomas Abdy defending Owen, who pleaded not guilty.

The prosecution summarised the case against Owen, outlining the discovery of the bodies, before allowing the witnesses to speak about seeing Owen in Marshall's clothes and being flush with money after the murders. Witnesses also testified that goods stolen from the Marshalls had been pawned in Uxbridge and Reading.

Dr Abdy had an unenviable task, but he did his best. He told the jury to disregard all that they had heard about Owen up to this point. He then highlighted four areas in which the case against Owen was weak. Firstly, he argued that there was no real evidence linking Owen to the scene of the crime at the time that the murders took place. He cast doubt on the value of Emma Simpson, who alleged she saw Owen walking from the direction of the Marshall's cottage. He poured scorn on the fact that just because Owen was wearing the clothes of the dead man that he must therefore have killed him. He also pointed to Owen's composure and stated that anyone who had committed such murders, and so faced the rope, could hardly remain so cool and collected as Owen had done.

The jury, though, remained unconvinced by the defence and found Owen to be guilty. According to *The Times*:

> He [Owen] listened to the sentence unflinchingly, saying with a military salute, 'Thank you, sir', and was removed amid the hisses of the audience. At the end of the case, the learned judge called for and passed a high eulogium on Superintendent Dunham, directing the authorities of the county to give him a £10 reward.

In the weeks following the passing of the death sentence, fresh facts came to light which illuminated Owen's motive. In 1867, Marshall had employed Owen to repair the wheels of a farmer's cart. Unfortunately, Owen botched the job and ended up burning the wheels in question. The owner refused to pay for the work, so Marshall did not pay Owen. A fight broke out and Marshall was assaulted, though Owen never received the money he thought he was entitled to. Apparently he vowed revenge and was heard to say, 'There is a man near Uxbridge who owes me some money and if I don't get it off him next time I go, I'll murder him.' This was repeated as he was about to be released from prison only two days before the murders.

There was a rival theory among the Marshall family, however. This was that Owen had determined to marry Mary Ann and so turned up just before the wedding was to occur. When she refused him, he killed the whole family. Yet this does not seem to tally with the known facts. After all, Owen arrived late at night, certainly not the time for a social call, and it is probable that he killed Marshall first.

It has already been noted that Owen had been the epitome of calm indifference throughout the trial, though some would call it callousness. Revd Bumberry, the prison chaplain, tried to make overtures towards the condemned man, but these were met with curses and foul expressions. Later, Owen claimed to be a Catholic, but when a priest was brought to see him, he behaved just as badly as he had with the chaplain, claiming that he did not believe there was a God. Nor did he feel any more charitable towards the police, stating, 'I am only sorry that I did not shoot Superintendent Dunham and a Justice of the Peace, that one who sentenced me as well.' When his aged father and estranged wife visited him in prison, he treated them coldly and responded to their tears with the question, 'What have you to snivel for?'

Just before his execution, Owen asked to sleep in the coffin that was made for him. Refusing to attend a last chapel service, he ate a hearty last dinner. After retiring at nine o'clock on the night before the execution, he slept soundly and woke at three the next morning. Whilst eating his breakfast he still asserted his innocence and joked with warders. The bell rang at eight and Owen's hands were tied as he met the hangman in the corridor. Once in front of the scaffold inside the prison grounds (public executions had ceased two years previously), he bounded up the steps two at a time. He then made a final address: 'My friends, I am going to die for the murder of Charles – What's his name? I forget. Oh! Charles Marshall: but I am innocent.' Owen's death was instantaneous.

Marshall did not leave a will but his goods on death, amounting to less than £100, were given to his son's aunt and guardian, Thurza Spooner, of Iver, when the will was proved in 1871.

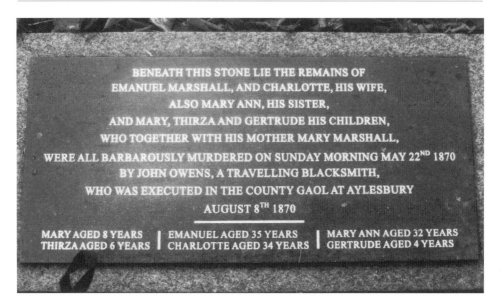

BENEATH THIS STONE LIE THE REMAINS OF
EMANUEL MARSHALL, AND CHARLOTTE, HIS WIFE,
ALSO MARY ANN, HIS SISTER,
AND MARY, THIRZA AND GERTRUDE HIS CHILDREN,
WHO TOGETHER WITH HIS MOTHER MARY MARSHALL,
WERE ALL BARBAROUSLY MURDERED ON SUNDAY MORNING MAY 22ND 1870
BY JOHN OWENS, A TRAVELLING BLACKSMITH,
WHO WAS EXECUTED IN THE COUNTY GAOL AT AYLESBURY
AUGUST 8TH 1870

| MARY AGED 8 YEARS | EMANUEL AGED 35 YEARS | MARY ANN AGED 32 YEARS |
| THIRZA AGED 6 YEARS | CHARLOTTE AGED 34 YEARS | GERTRUDE AGED 4 YEARS |

The commemorative plaque to the Marshall family.

The only consolation must be that Owen was caught quickly and paid with his life for his crimes. It should be said, too, that Owen was incredibly stupid. He could have escaped scot free, but for a number of foolish mistakes caused by greed and perhaps overconfidence. Having committed his crimes, he discarded his own clothes at the scene – clothes which he had been seen wearing and which could be identified as being his. Secondly, he took property belonging to Marshall, such as his clothes, his watch and his gun, and wore, pawned or kept these. All were recognised and thus betrayed him. Finally, he told Coombes where he was going and the latter led the police directly to him.

Sadly, young Francis Marshall, who escaped the massacre, died of TB in 1886 in Uxbridge.

6

A DOMESTIC MURDER

Olney, 1873

Throughout history, domestic murders have been, unfortunately, quite common, but the following is a most unusual example of that type of crime. It was deemed a most shocking crime at the time, as the local newspaper made clear. It stated:

> The remembrance of the Oving murder and the consequent execution has not died away, yet another wife murder has been added to the crimes for which this county has lately been notorious. The little town is in a state of painful and great excitement, for never within living memory, at all events had the dreadful crime of murder been committed before in its precincts.

Thrity-four-year-old Thomas Ward Nicholls was a shoemaker from Olney, a small town renowned for its shoe and bootmakers. He lived with his wife, Jane Hannah, a year his junior. Married in 1858, they had three children, all born in Olney; John aged four, Thomas aged nine, and Hannah, aged seven. They lived at Flood's Yard in Olney. It was the smartest house on the street and the only one to have a strip of garden at its front.

The family was respectable and Nicholls was highly regarded by all who knew him. His wife was from a family who was comfortably well off. However, she had spent all her share of the family money very soon after marriage. Nicholls usually attended Olney Baptist church, but his wife did not attend any place of religion. The minister, Revd J. Allen, said of him, 'He always appeared, to me, industrious and well conducted; he was a tolerably regular attendant.' Esther Crouch, a

The Baptist church at Olney.

neighbour who had known him all his life, said, 'I never knew anything wrong about Nicholls. He always seemed a good father and a good husband. He was sober from what I knew. I never saw him with a drink in all my life.'

Nicholls had served in the county militia in 1858. Major Hewett, Adjutant, recalled that he joined on 30 September 1858. He was so enthusiastic that on one occasion he even left the infirmary to attend militia training.

All was not well between man and wife, however. Apparently there were open affairs on both sides, and overindulgence in drink. This had not always been so on Nicholls' part, but recently he had indulged in courses, almost as reprehensible as those with which his wife was generally credited. Mrs Dicks, a neighbour, reported that:

His wife was a woman who liked a drop of drink sometimes. She was a good neighbour when she was solid and sober and when she kept from drink. She did not always keep from drink. When she was drunk she used bad talk. I remember her coming to me about half past twelve on the day of the murder. She said, 'I as drunk as . . .'

Esther Crouch's verdict was more lenient; 'His wife was a very good neighbour. She would have a little beer sometimes. I don't know that she was addicted to drink.' Police Sergeant Charles Batchelor said, 'I have seen both him and his wife in public houses but I never saw either of them drunk.'

Mrs Nicholls' character was not highly rated. On 11 October 1869, an effigy of her and two married men had been paraded around Mr Whitby's field, indicating that she was known to have committed adultery with both of them. Reverend Allen recalled that he had once heard that two men approached the Nicholls' house in December 1872, and one threw a stone at the window. Nicholls was not at home, but his wife was and she let them enter, dressed in her nightdress. Mrs Dicks said of Nicholls, 'I don't know he ever protected his wife when accusations were made against her.'

Nicholls' health was not good. He had been at the Northampton and Bedford Infirmary on a number of occasions. William Johnson, surgeon at the infirmary, recalled seeing Nicholls a few times between 1859 and 1872. In 1865, Nicholls had suffered from paralysis caused by consumption, and in 1872 he had been suffering from paralysis of the left side, possibly as a result of religious enthusiasm, which apparently equated to reading scriptures and singing hymns. Most recently, he had been collected from the Infirmary by his wife at the beginning of 1873. On his return, he visited an Anglican church to give thanks for his recovery, this being on the recommendation of the clergyman who had given him a letter of introduction for his most recent hospital visit.

In the week afterwards, he did little work. He and his wife argued, chiefly over her wanting to attend a village feast and Nicholls not wanting her to attend. This was probably because he feared she would get drunk there and meet undesirable men.

On Tuesday, 22 September 1873, Ann Chater, wife of Samuel Chater, a shoemaker of John Field's Yard, was employed by Mrs Nicholls as a washerwoman in their house. She had arrived at ten past seven in the morning and had breakfast at twenty past eight. Nicholls was working at home as usual. His wife left the house that morning to see her eldest son and her sister off from the railway station on the 10 a.m. train.

She was late in returning, so Nicholls asked his children to find her and bring her home. He also asked Ann if she knew whether his wife had been to Mill's (a beer shop) and she replied that she did not know.

Eventually, Nicholls left home himself and returned soon after, alone. He announced that his wife was at the pub, where she had had three pints of porter and a half pint of gin.

He returned to work, doubtless brooding on the wrongs his wife did to him, and plotting revenge. At one o'clock, his wife returned and the following dialogue ensued: 'Jane, what game do you call this? I won't have it.' He then hit her several times, before continuing, 'I'll draw the knife across your throat in a minute.' He then returned to his work, but continued addressing her, 'If you go with other people when I'm away, you shan't when I am here.'

'You – I'll go where I like. I won't live with you another day. You go to Sall Cooper again,' she said.

'Don't you tell me of that,' he replied.

She then said, 'You – I won't move, not if you kill me dead on the spot.'

Angry at her words, he said, 'I will do it. I am determined.'

With that, he took his wife by the neck and pulled her to the ground, then held her head back with his left hand and with his right he then cut her throat with his shoemaker's knife. She died quickly, as the weapon had cut her windpipe and several arteries. Two neighbours witnessed the murder and the children had dashed out to find help, shouting, 'Father will kill my mother, you are neighbours, why don't you come in?' And even though Esther Crouch arrived and pleaded, 'Oh, don't Tom, don't: pray, spare her life!' it had no effect.

A man named Childs went for help. He found George Horatio Grindon, a surgeon, riding on horseback nearby, and called on him to come with him to the scene of the crime. Grindon did so, as it was nearby. He found the dying woman, though there was nothing he could do for her. He also found the bloodstained knife.

Nicholls then left the house and found Police Sergeant Batchelor, to whom he reported his crime, saying, 'I have done it. It's drink! Drink! My poor head won't stand it as it used to.' Batchelor simply replied, 'I have heard so', for Childs had already told him what had happened. There was no evidence that Nicholls was drunk, or that he had had anything more than three cups of tea that day. His mother-in-law took the children away, while Batchelor took Nicholls to the police station at Newton Pagnell and detained him there.

On Tuesday 23 September, the inquiry took place at The Two Brewers Inn at Olney. Mr W.C. Davies, the deputy coroner for the northern district of the county, presided.

At the Magistrates' Court, on Wednesday, where Nicholls seemed depressed and made no defence, he was charged with murder and was committed for trial. The jury were obliged to see the scene of the crime, which was described thus:

On the floor, right in the doorway, clad in a dirty brown gown laid [*sic*] the body of the unfortunate victim of this deed. The head just inside the inner room, the feet in the outer kitchen. The body lay on its right side, the left arm laying naturally, the right one nearest the floor, extended at full length, with the fingers clenched. The hair was roughly disarranged. The features perfectly natural, and white as

The Two Brewers, Olney.

marble, stood out with painful distinctness from the bloodstained floor, and the eyes stared with a startled, terrified, horror-struck expression, not staring and vacant, but as still instinct with life. The windpipe and large blood vessels were severed and cut to the spine, and so savage was the wound that death must have been instantaneous.

Nicholls was conveyed to the county gaol by Inspector Hull on Thursday, 28 September. The trial took place at Aylesbury on 23 December, before Judge Honyman. Mr Monckton led for the Crown, and Mr Lathom Brook defended Nicholls. The defence claimed that Nicholls was not responsible for his actions, because he had suffered from consumption, rheumatism, epilepsy and paralysis. They suggested that his crime be reduced from murder to manslaughter.

The judge reminded the jury that it was deemed that the man was sane and so responsible for his actions, unless it could be proved otherwise. Provocation was only allowed if it had been more than verbal; in this case it was not so. The jury took just forty minutes to reach a verdict that Nicholls was guilty of murder, but they recommended him for mercy. The judge passed the death sentence, but also stated that the recommendation for mercy would be passed on.

The date for the execution was set at 8 a.m. on 12 January 1874. Nicholls was returned to Aylesbury gaol, where he suffered from two attacks of apoplexy, one of them quite serious. Meanwhile, petitions were signed and sent to the Home Secretary for a reprieve. Two were formulated in Aylesbury on his behalf. Among those who were prominent in his cause were the Revd Allen, two of the jurymen from the trial, a banker, a member of the Howard League, and many traders. The petitions were received on 29 December. On 5 January Nicholls' sentence was commuted to one of life imprisonment.

Nicholls was sent, initially, to Pentonville, and then to Princetown Prison on Dartmoor. He was released in the 1890s, however, he fell on hard times and by 1901 was an inmate in Newton Pagnell Workhouse. It is thought that he died in Newton Pagnell in 1918.

Pentonville Prison today.

7

DREADFUL MURDER AT SLOUGH

Slough, 1881

Slough has not had a good reputation amongst outsiders, largely thanks to John Betjemen's famous poem, *Slough*, but even before then, commentators were less than kind. In 1876, it was written, 'As a town, Slough has little to arrest attention. Of late years it has greatly increased in extent and population . . . The streets of Slough are lined with good shops and dwellings.' Seven years later, the county directory was a little more kind, 'Slough, which, but a few years since constituted of a few inns and other accommodation for traffic on the high road from London to Bath, is now a well built and rapidly increasing town, a polling station for the county and an important station on the Great Western Railway, being the junction of the Windsor branch.' In 1881 its population stood at just under 5,000.

One of the central streets, not far south from the railway station, was Windsor Road. Famous for being the home to The Observatory, residence of the Herschel family who once had the largest telescope in the world and were visited by George III, it also had a number of respectable residents, including a Major General and a magistrate, as well as a number of shops – one of which, from 1877, was a butchers ran by the Reville family. This shop was on the right-hand side of the road, fairly close to the High Street. In the shop part of the building was a board for chopping meat and a counter where the scales were kept. Behind that room was an office, including a desk with ledger, and a table for papers. Leading from there was a door to the kitchen and another door to the outside yard, which was only accessible from inside the shop. There were also stairs leading from the kitchen to the bedrooms upstairs.

The High Street, Slough, c. 1900.

Hezekiah Reville was born in Coton, Cambridgeshire, in about 1846. By 1861 the family lived in Bosham, Sussex, where he worked on his father's farm. Ten years later he lived with his brother-in-law at Horsham, where he was a butcher's assistant. In 1874 he married Ann, a year his senior, in Reading. They soon moved to Slough, which was where their two daughters, Alice and Emily, were born in 1875 and 1879.

They lived above their shop in Windsor Road, and husband and wife both contributed to the business, but they also employed others. One of these was Alfred Augustus Payne, a sixteen-year-old lad who lived with his family at the Royal Oak pub on the High Street. He had been born in Wexham, Buckinghamshire in about 1864, but moved with his family to Upton cum Chalvey in about 1866. He had worked for the Revilles for over two years and was able to write, as he had been seen writing a letter to his girlfriend. He usually began his day's work at seven in the morning and finished at eight o'clock at night. He was adept at using the chopper and used to slaughter sheep. Philip Glass was a butcher's boy of two year's service with the Revilles. Aged fourteen, he had been born in Slough and lived with his father, Alfred, a fly driver, and his mother, Mary Ann, both aged forty-nine, in Royal Cottages, Mackenzie Street.

All was not well in the household, though relations between husband and wife were smooth as far as was known. However, Phillip had heard Mrs Reville speak sharply to Payne, with the result that Payne had talked about handing his notice, but had been talked out of it by Mr Reville. These complaints were because Payne was allegedly spending too much time drinking in pubs rather than working, and often arrived late to work (a not uncommon complaint of employers about their youthful employees). However, though Philip Glass did not know of any recent complaint and certainly knew of no threat being spoken by Payne, Reville thought differently. He said that Payne had been neglectful of his work and Mrs Reville had had to speak to him on Sunday 10 April. It seems, though, that Mrs Reville had more grievances with Payne than her husband knew about. While Reville thought that Payne had stolen a rump steak, he wanted to be sure before tackling him on the topic, or to catch him in the act of dishonesty. His wife said, 'Oh, you'll never do that. You have not seen half of what I have seen.' She also thought Payne had had his hand in the till. Payne was not the only employee causing trouble. On the same Saturday, Reville had called on Mary Ann Glass, Philip's mother. He informed her that he had lost a quantity of steak and wondered whether her son had had anything to do with it.

On the evening of Monday, 11 April 1881, at about half past seven, Mary Callen of Arbour Vale arrived at the shop, and asked for a half-pound steak. She paid for it with a two-shilling piece, and Glass took the money before passing it to Mrs Reville. She was sitting in a chair in the inner room, working on the accounts. Her two daughters were asleep upstairs. It is uncertain when Reville, who had been at home all day, left her – accounts vary from 7.30 p.m. to 8.10 p.m. He went out to make some calls to James Wilmot's, a baker on William Street, and to Mr Green, before paying a visit to The White Hart pub on the High Street. Meanwhile, Glass had had his meal at 6 p.m. and stayed with Mrs Reville after her husband went out. So did Payne, though he spent some time rubbing some pickled hams as required. Glass left at about 8.20 p.m.; his colleague about ten minutes later.

Mrs Eliza Beasley, the next-door neighbour and wife of Alfred, a cooper, soon came to see Mrs Reville, as she often did, for company's sake. Mrs Beasley entered the shop by the front door, which was open, at about 8.30 p.m. or shortly afterwards. The gas light was burning and she could see through the shop to the room beyond it. She saw her friend, sitting in her chair, facing the window. A book was open on the desk. At first it seemed that she had fainted, but upon closer examination she found that her friend had been dealt two blows with a cleaver – one across her head and the other at the back of her neck.

Mrs Beasley called George John Laight, a coachbuilder, and another neighbour, and then left to find a policeman. Police Sergeant Hebbes, of the county constabulary, accompanied her back to the scene of the crime, arriving at about a quarter to nine. He saw the dead woman, who had actually been wounded in three places – two blows to the head and one to the neck – and her account book next to her, open on 19 March. On the floor there was some money, a pen, a handkerchief and splashes of blood. He then summoned medical assistance, but all that Dr William Urban Buce, surgeon and medical officer to the workhouse, could do upon arrival was to pronounce the poor woman dead. Dr Edward Dodd, surgeon and vaccinator of MacKenzie Street, also examined the corpse.

Superintendent Thomas Dunham, in charge at Slough police station, was called in to oversee the investigation. People remembered his triumph in his arrest of John Owen eleven years previously (see Chapter 5) and his stock stood high. A search of the premises was made, resulting in a strange note being found, which had been written on the back of an article about Rouen Cathedral taken from *The Builder*. It was addressed to Mrs Reville. It read: 'You never will sell me no more bad meat like you did on Saturday. I told Mrs Austin at Chalvey, that I would do for her. I done it for the bad meat she sold on Saturday last. H. Collins, Colnbrook.'

There was also a bloodstained cleaver, to which a human hair was attached. This was clearly the murder weapon.

The police called on Reville and informed him of his wife's murder; they also called on Payne's home too. Payne was asked if he knew about the murder, but he said not. However, he did not seem surprised once told of the news.

Initially, suspicion fell on the husband, but on finding that relations between man and wife were good, enquiries fell upon young Payne. He was apprehended at home that same night and taken to Slough police station.

The following day, the inquest was held at the Crown Inn on the High Street, but was soon adjourned to the petty session's court at the police station. Frederick Charsley, coroner for south Buckinghamshire, presided.

Payne, wearing his blue butcher's frock, gave evidence in the calmest possible manner. He said:

I've only got to say that Mrs Reville was sitting at the books when I came out of the door. She said 'Good night' to me and asked me if I should shut the door. She said, 'No, turn the gas down and leave the door open'. The tools were all laid together on the block when I came outside except the knife, and that lay out against the

Ann Reville's headstone. (Courtesy of Jean Smith)

weights and scale. It was 8.32 when I came out of the door, and I made straight home. I looked at the clock. That's all I've got to say. I don't want to say any more.

Reville was asked about the note and a customer called Collins, of Colnbrook. There was a Robert Collins of Chalvey who was a customer of Reville's and had had dealings with Payne and Glass, but he said that the note was not from him and nor had he complained about the meat from the shop. As to Mrs Austin, there was an Elizabeth Austin of Chalvey, but she did not know anyone with the name of H. Collins, nor had she complained about meat, nor did she ever deal with Payne. Jane Austin, also of Chalvey, also claimed she had no knowledge of the matter.

The inquest was adjourned for a week. Superintendent Dunham did not feel there was enough evidence against Payne to justify him being detained in police custody. He was, therefore, discharged. No one else was apprehended. However, because the body had been warm when seen by the doctor and because it had been discovered in a short amount of time following death, the window of opportunity for the killer had been very brief. Yet the evidence did not seem to point to anyone in particular.

At this point, there were various theories circulating. One was that the killing had been carried out by a tramp. The police, however, were more inclined to believe that Mrs Reville had been killed by someone she knew. This was because she had not risen from her chair on their entering the room, nor had she stopped working on the account books. Robbery did not seem to be a motive because little, if any, money was missing.

On a grim note, it later transpired that the first person to discover the corpse was actually one of Mr Reville's young daughters. On the day after the murder, Reville was informed by her that she had felt thirsty on the previous evening and so went downstairs to the kitchen to find a drink. She looked through the doorway into the office and saw the dead body of her mother and heard the front door slam. Terrified, she fled upstairs and lay awake until the next day.

The funeral took place on Thursday 14 April at six in the evening. Despite rain, a large procession followed the coffin as it left the house in Windsor Road and travelled south down the road to the parish church, St Mary's. The vicar, Revd Pownoll William Phipps, took the service and there were many floral tributes. Ann was buried to the south of the churchyard. Unusually for a murder victim, the headstone states that she was murdered.

Superintendent Dunham seemed at a dead end in the investigation, but he had sent the note found in the room to a handwriting expert, Mr Chabot of 27

Red Lion Street, London, to see if he could make anything of it. On Saturday 16 April, Dunham travelled to London to consult Chabot. He also met an analyst who had been checking Payne's clothes for any possible bloodstains. Finally, he consulted the CID.

His discoveries led him to feel confident that Payne was the killer. Dunham, Police Sergeant Hebbes and Mr Emanuel, a juryman, went to Payne's home, and at a quarter past six that evening, the youth was arrested in the presence of his father, Alfred. Dunham announced, 'It is my painful duty to charge you with a very serious offence, but before I do so I wish to caution you that whatever you may say I shall give in evidence whether it is for or against you.' Payne said nothing to this, but asked for a handkerchief and then went quietly to the police station. He had spent the afternoon with a friend in Windsor and was taken wholly by surprise at this new development.

The inquest was resumed on Tuesday 19 April, at the Magistrates' Court at Slough police station. The coroner stated that the additional evidence recently found by Dunham, especially that of the handwriting expert and the analyst, had to be examined. Payne was brought into court, but this time he stood in the dock, rather than the witness box, and, in comparison to his previous appearance, looked far graver.

By this time, Mr Reville and Philip Glass had apparently come under suspicion too, and it was felt that their movements on the night of the murder needed to be ascertained. Mr Reville claimed to have left home at between 7.45 and 7.50 p.m. He had walked northwards from Windsor Road to Wilmot's shop in William Street, remaining there for five minutes (Wilmot attested that this was true) before going to Richard Jenkins' greengrocer's shop on the same road, staying there for around ten minutes. He asked Jenkins whether he wanted to come with him for a drink and the two went to The White Hart. En route, they stopped at George Cornish's fancy repository on the same street for some tobacco. Jenkins could see him at all times when in Cornish's shop. They were drinking ale in the pub when Mr Harris' servant arrived and announced that Reville was wanted at home. Without drinking any more, he left.

Glass was called forward and reaffirmed his previous evidence. He was seen walking in the direction of the railway – thus walking away from the Reville's shop – by Kate Timms, a young woman who lived in the High Street. It was about 8.25 p.m. Ten minutes later she saw Payne by the Red Lion pub.

Other evidence as to Payne's movements that night came from George Rolfe, a brick maker from Slough Court. At about 8.30 p.m. he had seen Payne leave the Reville's shop. Rolfe addressed Payne, whom he knew, saying, 'Goodnight,

Gus,' and Payne replied, 'Goodnight George,', and walked northwards in the direction of the High Street. Payne closed the door behind him and Rolfe went home. Rolfe left shortly afterwards to go to the Grapes public house, further to the south on Windsor Road. As he passed the butchers for the second time, about seven minutes after seeing Payne, he did not notice anyone nearby. Other witnesses; neighbours Mrs Beasley and George John Laight, Police Sergeant Hebbes and Dr Dodd then repeated the evidence they had delivered previously.

Maria Barber, whose house adjoined that of the Revilles, also gave evidence. She had left home that evening at 8.20. She then saw Mrs Reville through the back window, but not Glass. Payne, however, was with her. She then left her house by the yard, which adjoined the two properties.

It was then the turn of Superintendent Dunham's new witness, Mr Chabot, who reported that on 13 April he had been given the mysterious note, along with a paper with Payne's name on it, and the following day received a sample of Mr Reville's handwriting and a specimen of Payne's. Finally, he was given an account book, which had both Reville and Payne's handwriting in it. He thought that the writing on the note was in a disguised hand. He did not think it was Mr Reville's handwriting, but that of Payne.

Evidence of Reville's innocence was given by Superintendent Dunham, who said that his coat had been examined for bloodstains, but none could be found. It should be noted that there was no reliable test for bloodstains at this date and it was easy for rust, dirt or food stains to be confused with bloodstains. Payne's shirt had two small specks of blood on it, but it was thought that these were some weeks old and had been caused when he was butchering a lamb.

Payne made the following statement:

All I have to say is that I am innocent of the crime. I knew nothing about it until Superintendent Dunham came to my house. He asked me to go to Mrs Reville and see where she was sitting when I left her at 8.32. When I accompanied Superintendent Dunham she did not appear to have moved an inch. Mr Reville says that I have some ill feeling against my last mistress, but I had not in the least. No two persons could agree better than me and Mrs Reville. Mr Reville said that I was in the habit of going to the public houses: for the last two months I have not. I gave it up as soon as he spoke to me about it. I should not have gone so much as I did had it not been for Mr Reville. I do not see how he could say that I was so bad after having given me so many presents.

The coroner decided that the inquest could now be concluded. He summed up all the evidence at length. He thought that the murder had not been committed by a stranger following Payne's departure from the shop, and that those people (presumably Mr Reville and Glass) to whom suspicion could be attached, had had their movements sufficiently checked and were cleared. He agreed with Chabot that the handwriting on the mysterious note was the same as Payne's. It was clear who he thought was guilty. The jury retired at 4.15 p.m. and took two hours discussing the matter. They returned with the verdict that Payne was guilty, though with one member of the jury dissenting.

On 20 April, at a meeting of the Slough Petty Sessions, the solicitor for Payne did not cross-examine the witnesses. Instead it was Dr Dodd who was given more prominence. He said that any of the blows found on the deceased could have rendered her unconscious. He thought that the wound at the back of the head had been the first one inflicted and that the assailant had been standing behind his victim.

Payne did not have long to wait to discover his fate. Murder cases were heard at the assizes of the Midland Circuit, and the next hearing was at Aylesbury on 28 April, where there were two murder trials taking place. He was indicted for murder and pleaded not guilty, though when he stood in the dock he did so with an air of indifference. Mr Reville was called upon to give evidence. The only new points he made was that the house could be entered by the gate of the yard, but that it was impossible to open from the outside unless the person was well acquainted with its manipulation by a piece of string.

All this was looking pretty black for Payne. Yet Maria Beasley's evidence seemed more favourable towards him. She recalled returning home that evening and finding the gate of the yard between the two houses open. It was certainly opened by someone from the inside, but George Rolfe had seen Payne leaving by the front door of the shop. The evidence had all been given, but the judge, Mr Justice Lopes, delayed the summing up until the following day.

The trial was continued and concluded on the morning of 29 April. Mr Chabot provided his evidence as to the handwriting being that of Payne's, judging by the specimens of Payne's writing provided. Yet Mr Attenborough, defending Payne, argued that it could not be certain that the specimens of writing were those of Payne's. He added that Glass had believed them to be so, but there was no certainty. It was also observed that there was no blood found on Payne's clothes, that he had no strong motive, and that no money had been found on his person, as it was possible that Mrs Reville might have been robbed of what little she had on her. He also argued that the case against Payne rested in the slender fact that it seemed impossible for anyone else to have committed the crime, rather than on any positive evidence against Payne. He said that the eight minutes between Payne leaving and the discovery of the body was ample time for someone else to have killed Mrs Reville. He also added that it was not known whether Payne knew of the people mentioned in the note, because if he did not then he could not possibly have been the author.

After the judge summed up the case, the jury left to deliberate. They were quick in coming to their verdict, taking a mere half hour to do so. They found that Payne was not guilty of the murder, and the young man left the court, acquitted.

No one else was ever charged with the murder of Mrs Reville and her murder went unsolved. Was Payne fortunate or was he innocent? Certainly the circumstantial evidence against him seemed strong. He had had disagreements with his employers and was the last to see Mrs Reville alive as far as is known. It would not have taken him long to have taken the unsuspecting woman by surprise, to have dealt the fatal blows and then to have left by the front door.

On the other hand, it is possible that someone else might have been guilty. Philip Glass might have had had a motive, though his differences seem to have been with Mr Reville, not his wife. However, he left the shop before Payne and was seen some distance away minutes later, his opportunity seems to have been limited. Reville, too, came under suspicion, but his movements after leaving his wife to the discovery of her body seem accounted for by a number of witnesses. Or was the killer a burglar, referred to by Maria Barber, who had apparently been in her house the previous week? He could have left by the yard as the gate was open and no one else is known to have opened it. Perhaps, upon seeing the chopper, the man used it to silence Mrs Reville and left before he could affect any robbery? Yet Mrs Reville had not left her chair, which she surely would have done if the man was a stranger to her.

It seems that the truth will never be known for certain. The police suspected Mr Reville, Glass and Payne, but mostly the latter. They had no other suspects and no stranger was seen. The probability is that Payne was guilty and it seems a very far-fetched coincidence that someone, almost certainly known to the victim, could have waited for him to leave and then gone in and committed the murder. Clearly the jury gave him the benefit of the doubt.

Mr Reville moved to Brighton after the murder, sometime between 1883 and 1887, living at 17 Southover Street with his daughter, Alice, and two servants. He was now running a bakery. In 1913, he married Alice Tullett, and died in Brighton in 1933. Glass and Payne were still residing in Slough ten years after the murder; both now married men. However, as with their former employer, neither was employed in the butchering trade, with Glass working as a fly driver (following in his father's footsteps) and Payne as a labourer. Whatever secrets they harboured about the murder of Mrs Reville, they took them to their graves.

Emily Reville is known to have been married in Brighton in 1908.

8

LUCKY ESCAPE?

Bledlow, 1893

Forensic science is now seen as one of the major elements of criminal investigation, but in the nineteenth century it was relatively rudimentary. This prevented many otherwise successful criminal cases from reaching fruition. As Sherlock Holmes told Dr Watson in 1881:

> Criminal cases are continually hinging upon that one point. A man is suspected of a crime . . . His linen or clothes are examined and brownish stains are discovered upon them. Are they bloodstains, or mud stains or rust stains, or fruit stains, or what are they? That is a question which has puzzled many an expert, and why? Because there was no reliable test?

This case was one of them; the ultimate question being whether two killers escaped justice because of it.

John Kingham was a farmer who lived in Newell's Farm, Bledlow Ridge, three miles from Princes Risborough, with his grandson, Herbert, then aged twelve and a half. Kingham was born in 1828, and, in 1862, was married to Susannah Gregory from North Marston, who was seven years his senior. The couple had at least two sons and one daughter together. In 1861, he was an agricultural labourer and Susannah was a lace maker, living in Common Lays. In 1881, he was a farmer at Newell's 44-acre farm, near Yewsden Wood, which was owned by Lord Carrington. By 1891, he was separated from his wife, who referred to herself as a widow. Kingham cooked for himself and his grandson, but a local woman, Mrs Dorcas Martin, come in each morning to do the housework, whilst her husband, George, worked on the farm for Kingham. Kingham himself was known for being a steady and industrious man, yet the life of this apparently respectable man was about to about to be cut short in a most terrible fashion.

Initially, some newspapers reported that Kingham and his grandson had been attacked on the road after hearing shots, but the true facts of the case soon emerged. He was last seen alive on the early evening of Thursday 28 September. His grandson recalled:

> I lived with him. No one else lived in the house with us. I last saw him alive at half past five o'clock on the evening. He was, then, out behind chopping wood. It was not very often that he went out in the evenings. I went out to play at half past five, and when I got back at a quarter to eight I found he was not at home. I went into the house and lit a light, and found he was not there. I then went out and saw that the cow had not been milked, and that he had not been into the stable to give the horses any hay. They had not had anything since [George Martin] went away. I went down to George Martin's, getting there about half past eight. Mrs Martin is the woman who comes in every morning to see to the housework. We stopped there a little while, and then Mrs Martin said her husband better come over to see if he could milk the cow. He did go and let the calf loose to the other one. We did not tell the policeman until next morning. Mrs Martin, a girl and I happened to go down to the wood where he was found, but only to the upper part of the wood. We did not hear any shots. We came home and sat in the house ever so long, and then I went down to Martins' to sleep. It was just about twelve o'clock when we got to bed. The next morning George Martin gave information to PC Ware. My grandfather was not in the habit of going out – he never went out unless he was obliged to.

George Martin had seen Kingham alive and well at ten past five, leaving the farm with a bundle of hazel wood under his arm. He searched part of the wood from 10 p.m. until 2 a.m. Then Mrs Martin and Jonah Britnell, publican of the nearby pub The Boot, searched for three hours afterwards.

PC Ware was approached by Mr Martin and Britnell early on Friday 29 September. The village constable recalled:

> On Friday morning I received information that the deceased was missing, and went in search of him. I found his body in Yewsden Wood, lying about twenty-five yards from the footpath leading up to what they call Bellows Hill Field, in the middle

Yewsden Wood.

of the wood. The footpath went from Radnage Bottom and through Bellows Hill Field. It was about twenty past seven in the morning when I found him. I was in the company of two men, Jonah Britnell and George Martin. The deceased's head was inclining a little to the right. He had a bruise on the forepart of his head, and a slight cut below the left eye, as from a blow. His skull was fractured in two places at the back, and his throat was cut. His hat was lying about three quarters of a yard from him . . . he was very wet all over, but there was no appearance of a struggle. The ground was covered with leaves, but the leaves did not seem disturbed. It had been wet during the night and the rain may have rinsed some of the blood away. There was a little blood on the boughs near, and a good deal of blood on the back of the deceased's head.

The policeman guarded the body and sent Jonah Britnell to summon senior police officers from High Wycombe. On the way he met John Avery, who asked, 'What do you want?' Britnell replied, 'Kingham's found in the wood with his throat cut'. 'Oh God,' answered Avery.

They returned to the scene together, Avery carrying a shotgun. He did not stay long and was asked by the constable to bring some sacks back with him.

91

Britnell left too, to summon the police from High Wycombe. The police found a nail and some string in the pockets of the deceased, but no money or weapon.

Dr Charles Fortescue Pridham, a surgeon from Stokenchurch, arrived at the scene of the crime and made some discoveries after an examination of the corpse. He found:

> An extensive wound across the front of the throat, about two inches long. It completely divided the windpipe and some large blood vessels on the right side. I also found a small punctured wound on the side of the right ear, and a large wound on the upper back of the head on the right side, extending to the brain substance. From that wound the skull was fractured nearly the whole of the right side. There was also an injury on the lower part of the back of the head on the right side of the skull and was also fractured there. There were spots of blood on the face from the nose, and also on the backs of the hands. The wound on the throat was inflicted by an instrument such as a knife, and a very strong one. A heavy blunt instrument caused the injury to the back of the head.

The doctor believed that Kingham had been attacked by either two people, each striking once with the butt of a gun, or one person striking twice, and that the throat had been cut after the blows had been struck to Kingham's head. He noted that there was not much blood on the ground as it had been soaked up by the mud around it. He could not state when death occurred.

Superintendent John James Maneely arrived from High Wycombe at ten past nine that morning. He had the corpse removed to Newell's Farm. That afternoon he met John Avery, who was not, at this point, a suspect. Avery was a forty-seven-year-old agricultural labourer, born in Bledlow Ridge. He now lived in Bennet End, Radnage, with his seventy-seven-year-old widowed mother, Mary Ann, his twin brother, Richard, who was also an agricultural labourer. Richard had married a woman named Ellen who was twenty years his junior in 1892, and they had a baby son, Henry. In their younger days, both brothers had been chair makers and lived in Bledlow.

Avery made the following voluntary statement:

> Yesterday afternoon, at about half past four, I went along to Cross Lane Pond. I had a gun with me. As I stood by the farm I heard two shots fired up in the wood. I stopped there a little while. I often went along the lane as far as Radnage churchyard, and while I was standing in the churchyard, I heard two other shots fired. I could then hear people talking quite plain and I could tell from their voices who they were.

St Mary's churchyard wall, Radnage.

Radnage Church.

When pressed to identify these people, he became rather shy, saying, 'It is hard to swear to voices and I would not like to do so.' On the following day, the police arrested John Avery. He then remembered who he had heard on the Friday, claiming that one of the voices belonged to Jim Brooks, known as 'Patsy' Brooks. The police also searched Avery's home and found bloodstains on his clothing, together with pheasant's feathers and a knife. When he saw the police with the knife, he replied, 'You will find none of the old man's blood on that.'

The inquest began on Saturday 30 September at The Boot pub in Bledlow Ridge. George Fell was the coroner, and called Susannah Kingham as the first witness. She was not terribly upset about her husband's death, stating, 'The deceased man was my husband. He was a farmer. His age was about 57. He lived in Newell's Farm, near this house. I have not lived with him for sometime. I have seen the body the jury have viewed and identified it as my husband.'

Young Herbert then gave his evidence. He told the inquest: 'I had just gone away from him and got down to the white gate. I heard a gun in the direction of the wood at the time. It seemed in the direction of the wheat field.' He did not hear any more shots. PC Ware produced a stick belonging to Kingham, which was found near to the corpse. There was a little blood on the stick. Motive was unclear, as he stated, 'I have no actual knowledge of there being any ill feeling towards the victim. He was a civil, quiet, harmless man.' All he could suggest was that some people might object to a man who owned property and had a little money.

The coroner noted that this was a case of murder, but at half past three that afternoon, he adjourned the inquest because the enquiry was ongoing.

On Tuesday 3 October, Majors Hewitt and Powell, two county magistrates, held the first day of the investigation in High Wycombe police station. It was of great interest to the public and a large crowd waited outside; especially interested that John Avery was brought before the magistrates. The superintendent called for the suspect to be remanded in custody as the enquiry proceeded and more evidence was gathered against him. After Avery had spoken, his solicitor, Mr Robert Samuel Wood of High Wycombe, opposed the police request, but was turned down and Avery was sent to Reading Prison.

In the meantime, PS Hobley arrested Avery's brother, Richard, who was described as a tall, spare man. Bloodstains had been found on his clothing too – on his trousers and his shirt. He assured the police that this had been caused when he was skinning a lamb on the Sunday after the murder and protested his innocenc: 'That shirt I was wearing last Sunday and the blood I account for. I helped skin some sheep for Mr Horwood of Lodge Hill Farm. The blood on the shirt was before I turned my sleeve up and that on the trousers as he burst and came over me.' Still, he was taken to High Wycombe police station on Hughenden Road.

On 12 October, both brothers were charged with murder at the Magistrates' Court. Their solicitor protested that there had been attempts made by the prison staff to get at them and to force them to make incriminating statements. The magistrates deplored these accusations and the police denied that they had behaved in such a manner.

Herbert Kingham spoke again. He stated that, 'He did tell me someone had threatened him . . . it was when he was summoned about twelve months ago.' The case in question had been against Brooks, who was mentioned earlier by John Avery as the man heard near Yewsden on the Friday evening. Mr Horwood had summoned Brooks for poaching and Kingham had been a witness against him. Brooks later said, 'This is not done for nothing – someone will have to die for it.' Yet Brooks had an alibi for the murder, and various witnesses testified to having seen the Avery brothers near the wood on the day of the murder. Uriah Dell saw John near the wood after hearing shots there, and Daniel Oxley saw Richard with a gun shortly after hearing shots near the wood. Elizabeth Styles of Radnage had seen Kingham enter the wood at a quarter to six, and then heard some shots. The Averys were remanded in custody once again.

The next court hearing was a week later, on 19 October. There was some relief for the Averys, as Herbert stated, 'I never heard them threatening grandfather. They were good friends as far as I know and made occasional visits.' Likewise, Thomas Howard, who employed Richard for farmwork and as a gamekeeper, recalled having him investigate shots in the wood, but that he did not know him to carry a gun on these occasions. William Claydon, a farmer of Hill Farm, Bledlow, recalled seeing Richard on the evening of the murder, but only saw that he had manure, not blood, on his shirt.

At the next hearing, a week later, the question of Kingham's hat and stock were brought up. These had been found near the corpse, and though the police had taken them into their possession, they did not think they were important as evidence. They were now missing. There were also questions asked about the time of death, but no precise time could be given, only that the body was cold and stiff when found.

Mr W.W. Fisher, a coroner's analyst of Oxford, had examined the clothing taken from the Averys, which he had received on 4 October and had returned eight days later. Yet his evidence was inconclusive. Yes, there was a bloodstain on the inside of the jacket, but the hairs there were those of a partridge and of a hare. There were spots of blood on other clothes, but there were none on the knife, gun or boots. These traces of blood were human, not animal, and were about two weeks old. Fisher concluded, 'Some of the spots are not consistent with a man wearing it when committing murder, others may be.' The relative primitive state of what would now be called forensic science did not further the investigation one jot.

Other witnesses gave statements about the Averys, all of whom said they had seen them in the woods nearby on the evening of the murder. One saw Richard at ten to six, but he did not have a gun, and nor was he bloodstained. Charles Rogers said he saw Daniel Brooks and Richard Avery at a quarter to six and that they heard shots, with the latter remarking, 'They be at the pheasants again.' Constance Goodchild remembered seeing a man who had his back to her, enter the wood between five and six o'clock, armed with a gun; 'The man was tall, but I do not know who he was.'

The magistrates retired at ten past seven to discuss whether there was a case to be brought against the Avery brothers, which could be tried at the Assizes. They came to a conclusion within minutes and the chairman relayed their message to the two men:

> Your case has been thoroughly investigated as far as the prosecution is concerned, and the duty of the magistrates is to satisfy that there is a *prima facie* case to send forward to put you in trial for this serious offence. Well, as you know, and as a great many others here know, we have spent a good many hours over this case. We have thoroughly gone into it, and the case which me and my brother magistrates came to, is that there has not been sufficient evidence advances to satisfy them to put you upon your trial, and therefore you will be dismissed. But, clearly understand that it does not relieve you if any further evidence is brought against you. You will be liable to be taken up upon the same charge, and have to stand your trial perhaps then. But at present there is not sufficient evidence to satisfy the magistrates, who now hear your case to send it forward to put you on your trial.

In the streets, the brothers were alternatively hissed and cheered, clearly reflecting the division of opinion whether they were rightly dismissed or not. They then went home with their mother, John Avery's wife, other relatives and friends.

There is no definitive conclusion to this tale. Were the Averys guilty but escaped justice because of the lack of conclusive evidence? They certainly seem to have had the opportunity to kill Kingham, as they were in the vicinity of the wood at the right time. But that was all. There was no obvious motive or ill feeling between them and Kingham, and there was no other evidence.

9

CHILD MURDER AT COLNBROOK

Colnbrook, 1900

Murder is always foul, but surely the killing which is most abhorrent is that of a child. Mercifully these are very rare, and when they do occur, they are usually the work of someone known to the child, often a family member. Stranger danger, which is so often preached about, is relatively unusual. But it is not unknown, as this case will tell.

William Smith, a bricklayer, and Harriett Maria, his wife, had lived with their five children in a house in Poyle Road, Colnbrook for two-and-a-half years in 1900. The Smiths were poor; William was a labourer, and had many mouths to feed.

On the morning of Friday, 17 August 1900, Mrs Smith sent her eight-and-a-half-year-old daughter, Elizabeth (Lizzie) to do some shopping for her. Lizzie was described as being pretty, intelligent and with brown hair and brown eyes. Firstly, she was sent out with some money to buy some rashers of bacon for her father's breakfast, returning at five to eight. She then ate a breakfast of bread and jam and drank tea. Her father – who had already been at work – returned home for breakfast, eating between eight and half past.

Later that morning she went to the Golden Cross pub to fetch her father some beer to accompany his dinner. At 11.30 a.m. she ran another errand, this time to Mrs McGregor's at Colnbrook, about half a mile away. She was given a shilling to buy sixpence of bacon and a tin of black-lead at Stubling's, the grocers. She was told by her mother to make haste because the bacon was for her father's dinner. And that was the last time that Mrs Smith saw her daughter alive.

Three girls saw Lizzie on her way to the shop. Firstly, Daisy Cranham saw her outside Mr Alexander's house. 'Are you coming with me to McGregor's?' Lizzie asked Daisy, to which she replied, no, she had to look after the Star and Garter pub. Nellie Alexander saw Lizzie at about noon and greeted her, but her friend did not hear her. Ellen Barnes also saw her turning the corner by the Punch Bowl pub.

By lunchtime, Mrs Smith was becoming very worried, as her daughter should have been home by then. Her husband told her not to be, saying that she might be at one of her aunts' houses in Colnbrook. But when she did not return, Mrs Smith went in search of her husband, who had by then returned to work, and at twenty to five, told him that she feared their daughter might have got lost. He told the village constable, PC Young, who in turn told Smith that he would inform him of any relevant news. Smith and his wife began to search for themselves. Mrs Smith called on the aunts, but they could not tell her anything. Smith walked about the streets, looking for his daughter.

The weekend passed without any sign of the missing girl. On Monday morning, John Richard Wootton, a 22-year-old ex-Merchant Navy man and now a gardener, gave Smith the news he feared. He did not know Lizzie personally, but he often gave cart rides to her crippled brother.

That morning he had to go to the Paper Mill shed. This was latched but not locked, so anyone could have access to it. Inside were large bales of paper, each weighing 2cwt. When Wootton arrived, the door was wide open. He saw a straw hat just over the threshold. Picking it up, he saw bloodstains. He then saw the sole of a shoe sticking out from beneath a bale. Having heard a description of the missing girl, he recognised it as hers, but he did not want to investigate further by lifting the bale. The man left the shed and saw one Charles Strong, but did not inform him of the news because he did not think he should do so. Wootton found Smith and the following conversation took place.

'You're just the man I'm looking for,' said Wootton.

'What's up then?' asked Smith.

'Don't make yourself alarmed, but I believe the child's in the shed.'

'Is she dead or alive?'

'I believe she's dead. I've see'd the hat and I've saw the sole of her boot underneath some bales of paper.'

Once Smith had learnt this terrible news, he broke down. He then went for help.

The police were called and PS Chamberlain, who was in the neighbourhood, gave Wootton a note to take to Staines police station, to summon Sub Divisional Inspector Unstead and Inspector Arrow of the CID. They searched the land around the shed for footprints and other clues, but none were found. However, inside the shed they found a number of gas pipes, some fifteen inches long. One

The Golden Cross pub.

The Punch Bowl pub.

had bloodstains on it. There were also cigarette boxes there. No money or bacon rashers were found on the corpse.

Dr Albert James Southey of North Crawley was also summoned. He knew Lizzie, and arrived at ten past nine. He had the body moved from the shed so he could see her more clearly, and the position that the corpse had been found was noted. She was lying flat on her face, doubled-up, with her right leg straight and left leg bent. Her skull had been fractured by severe blows to the head by a blunt instrument. There were also cords about her neck, but these had not caused her death. It was possible that one of the gas holders in the shed had been used to kill her. Later, at the post-mortem, he found that there were no signs of food in her stomach. She had not been raped and had probably been killed in the shed itself, probably on the day she disappeared.

A suspect was detained almost immediately. He was never named, but he was able to give a satisfactory account of himself, so was released on the same day. On Tuesday a more promising suspect was located – George Taylor, a thirty-eight-year-old labourer.

On 20 April 1897, Taylor, described as a man of the tramping class, had been seen with the then five-year-old Lizzie by the riverbank at Horton. Her seven-year-old brother, William Alexander, alerted their mother and Mrs Smith ran across the fields, hearing her daughter scream. Lizzie ran to her; her clothing was torn. Mrs Smith went to the Five Bells pub at Horton to fetch her husband. He and others from the pub went in pursuit of Taylor, whom they apprehended and had arrested. Smith said, 'What have you done to my daughter, you scoundrel?' Taylor's reply was, 'Alright, I'll go with you, but it is a false charge.' Dr Southey examined the girl and found she had not been subject to any violence. Nevertheless, Taylor was tried on 19 June at the assizes for indecent assault. William and Lizzie both testified against Taylor. Taylor pleaded not guilty, but put up no defence. He was found guilty and sentenced to six months in gaol, with hard labour. Yet, although (in 1900) the police investigated Taylor's activities for the few days leading up to the murder, they could not find that he had any opportunity to commit the hideous crime. He was released without charge.

The inquest was held on Wednesday 22 August, at the White Hart Hotel. Dr Gordon Hogg, the coroner for West Middlesex, presided. Firstly, the jury had to view the corpse at the paper mill. Then Mrs Smith identified the body and explained what she had witnessed on the day of her daughter's disappearance. The deceased's father and John Wootton gave their evidence of the discovery of the body. Other witnesses were called and gave their evidence. However, the jury could only conclude that this was a case of murder by person or persons

The White Hart House.

unknown. Finally, it was stated that the Smiths had very little money to cover funeral expenses, but a subscription was formed and money was promised to help them.

On Thursday, 23 April at 8 p.m., Lizzie's funeral took place. The coffin was borne by six members of the Poyle Congregational Church's Sunday school, which Lizzie had been a member of. Family and friends followed the funeral procession. Hymns were sung and scripture read. Then the procession went to St Thomas' Church, where she was buried in the churchyard. The many floral tributes laid by the grave were a silent testimony to the great sympathy which local people felt for the Smiths.

Lizzie's mother said that she could not account for the murder, and suggested that it was her daughter's fate. She had dreamt that her daughter had been accosted by two gypsies, kidnapped and knocked about, before the dream ended. Her father had additional unpleasant experiences:

I feel almost broken-hearted. What do you think I have been obliged to hear? Why, as I was coming home, people asking me whether they had let me out, and

St Thomas' Church, Colnbrook.

whether I was on bail or whatever. It is bad enough to lose the poor child without it being spread about that I had been arrested, and that me and my wife were about to be charged with the murder. Why I love my children dearly . . . and they love me.

A fortnight after the murder, forty-year-old Gustavus Reginald Peat, from Sweden, was arrested for theft. He had previously spent a fortnight at Staines Union Infirmary as a lunatic, but was released as cured. He had been working on a farm on Staines Moor on the evening of 17 August. He stole a pick handle worth sixpence, which belonged to Thomas Henderson, a Staines baker.

At the Magistrates' Court he was said to be homeless, but he claimed he was a householder and a vestryman in the London parish of Pimlico, Ebury Bridge, with a wife and five children. There was laughter and disbelief in court, yet this was true – though he had been missing from home for seven weeks. He was remanded in custody and was next seen at Teddington Magistrates' Court.

The charge of the theft of the pick handle was dropped. A more serious charge was now levelled against him; that of killing Lizzie Smith. Bloodstains were found on his clothes and he had cigarette boxes of the same type that police found in the shed on 20 April. He had also been seen with a piece of lead piping.

Peat made a number of statements. Firstly he said:

I live at Peabody Buildings, Ebury Bridge, Pimlico. I am a general labourer and left my home in search of work. The last time I saw my wife she refused me admittance. She suffers with the family complaint – which is lunacy . . . I was once detained in an asylum in 1894, and on several other occasions. I have worked for the past seven years to bring about a reform of the lunacy laws . . . on Thursday I slept on a farm near Wraysbury station . . . Next morning I had some work on another farm, from which I received 7½ d. When I left, I lost my way . . . The bacon was given to me by a man at the farm. I have made a practice of carrying pieces of iron piping with me as a means of defence when going about . . . I love blood – the blood of Sacrament.

He was then charged with the murder of Elizabeth Smith, to which he replied:

That is nothing more than what I expected. I shall not withdraw anything I have said – not a word. Small charges, as a rule, have a witness. They cannot investigate a case against a prisoner who has not been seen to commit the crime. I might charge you with committing the murder. I would rather be hanged for a crime committed when I had my senses then I would hang for a crime committed when insane in the estimation of others.

Peat was committed to trial at the Old Bailey in London. He then said:

If you can say I am guilty you must prove your case. Why should I say whether I am guilty or not? I thank you for your hearing, and particularly the witnesses, who are the public in court. I am fighting your causes. I want to bring home to the working classes that circumstantial evidence will hang a man.

The trial took place at the Central Criminal Court on 20 November, before Mr Justice Darling. Peat was charged with murder. The jury were sworn in and had to discern whether the accused was of sound mind and so fit to plead to the indictment. Dr Scott, the medical officer, had had Peat under observation since 7 September, and he considered Peat to be insane; that he was suffering from chronic mania. He thought that the prisoner had some, but not a complete, understanding of the charge against him. He did not think he was mentally capable of pleading or defending himself. Peat denied this on the grounds that he thought the doctor had not seen him for long enough to make a judgement, as he had only spoken to him for half an hour. Dr Scott said that he had studied his conduct and correspondence for long enough to know. Peat persisted in saying Scott might be in error, and that if he was accused of murder, he *should* be tried. Yet the jury decided that Peat was not of sound mind, and so was incapable of pleading. Therefore, the judge ordered that Peat be sent to Broadmoor.

It is not known when Peat was released from Broadmoor, but he died in East Retford, Nottinghamshire in 1917.

The known evidence against Gustavus Peat was limited to the fact that he was in the locality at the time of the murder, that he had bloodstains on his clothing, carried piping and cigarette boxes of the type found near Lizzie's corpse. It seemed enough, however. We do not know the motive for the murder, either. She was not killed for financial gain, or for obvious sexual purposes. Possibly insanity was to blame. It seems the truth will never be known.

10

THE SECOND
SLOUGH MURDER

Slough, 1910

We have already examined the murder of a female shopkeeper in Slough, which occurred in 1881 (see Chapter 7). We will now look at one which took place almost three decades later, though this case had a rather different result than that of Mrs Reville. Slough was a rather different place than it was in 1881, too; it was far bigger and, with a population of about 9,500 in the 1901 census, was the second most populous town in the county, second only to High Wycombe.

Mrs Isabella Wilson had been born in Towcester, Northamptonshire, in 1840. In the 1860s she had married Richard Wilson, of Maidenhead. In 1871 they were living in London Road, Bracknell, and in 1881 at 64 Alpha Road, Kingston. Then they lived at various addresses in Ealing between 1886 and 1896, including Grove Place, Baker's Lane and Singapore Terrace, all in the poorer parts of the town. They do not appear to have had any children; certainly none that survived infancy. Wilson was a chimney sweep for most of this time, though by 1895 he was a dealer in second-hand furniture. He died in January 1896, aged fifty-eight, and by 1901 his widow was living at 14 Dellary's Road in Surbiton, working as a wardrobe purchaser, later moving to St Leonard's Street, Windsor. From about 1904 she had resided in Slough, running a second-hand clothes shop at 22 High Street. This was in a block of three shops. At No. 20 was a branch of Singer's, selling sewing machines, and at No. 18 was Mr Robert's tobacconists. Mrs Wilson was described as a good businesswomen with a kindly disposition, and was doing fairly well. However, she did have her worries. Her weekly rent was 12s and sometimes there were problems in paying it. She did wonder about applying for an old age pension, and also in giving up the business due to her age.

Isabella's health was described as being good, however, the eyesight in one of her eyes was very poor. Her sister sometimes helped out, as did her neighbours. She was reserved about her private life. Fatally, she did not bank her takings; as her sister said, 'She used to carry a good deal of money about with her, wrapped in paper.'

Mary Ann Holton, a widow and a friend of Mrs Wilson, also stated, 'I have seen her wrap gold in paper and put it in the satchel purse. I have also seen her wearing the watch chain . . . She wore a gentleman's silver watch.' She had also been seen paying bills with sovereigns. It is unlikely that she took much money from the people who were obliged to buy second-hand clothes, but even so she was evidently seen as a target worth robbing, because she carried a relatively large amount of money on her person. It was stated in the press in 1910 that, 'She often had rough characters in her shop after clothes.'

Mrs Wilson often lay down on the sofa in her living room between 1 and 2 p.m. each afternoon. This room was just off from the shop and she would usually keep the door open so she could see any potential customers. She had lived with her sister, Mariah, since arriving in Slough, until the latter married Edward Henry White, a retired Windsor coal merchant, three years previously. They lived in Ivydene, King Edward Street, Slough. Following her sister's marriage, Mrs Wilson lived alone – though the Whites saw her about two or three times a week, often in the evenings.

On 30 June, Mrs Wilson said that about three weeks prior, a stranger asked her if she would settle down with him, but nothing more came of this marriage proposal. On Thursday 14 July, the Whites visited her as usual. Mrs White later said of her sister that, 'she was very cheerful and very nice'. They talked for an hour.

Mrs Wilson was last seen alive at 11 a.m. by Mrs Kent, wife of the landlord of The Forester's Arms, the pub opposite her shop. She recalled seeing Mrs Wilson 'In her shop, putting a pair of brown boots in her window.'

That afternoon, Henry Bright, a milkman, made his delivery. He recalled:

About four o'clock on Friday afternoon I went to Mrs Wilson's shop as usual. As she was not in the shop I knocked on the counter, but could get no reply. As the old lady was very deaf, I took no notice of this, but put the milk on the counter, and then noticed three pence on the floor. That being the amount due to me, I picked it up, thinking she had put it on the counter for me and it had slipped off. Everything seemed as usual about the shop, so I took no notice of the old lady's not answering to my knock.

Slough high street, c. 1900s. (Courtesy of Paul Lang)

Mr Roberts, the tobacconist next door, heard nothing untoward that day, despite the fact that Mrs Wilson's back door had been open all day, which was unusual.

The Whites left their home at seven o'clock to do their shopping, but also to call on Mrs Wilson. Edward White recalled what happened next:

We arrived there at about twenty past seven [in the evenning], but when we got opposite the shop we saw a motor-bicycle outside. The handles of the machine were resting against the window, and thinking it was a customer [this individual was never identified, but was clearly not the killer as death had occurred in the early afternoon] engaged in the shop we did not go in, but decided to do our shopping first and call back on the old lady. We had been to see her the night before and she was all right.

At about eight o'clock we returned, when the shop door was open as usual, and the motor-bicycle was gone. As soon as we got into the shop we noticed that the middle door entering the sitting room was nearly closed. This was unusual, as Mrs Wilson always kept it open so she could see into the shop. When we saw that the door was closed we wondered what the matter was, and I called out, thinking she might have gone to sleep. There was no answer, and on pulling the door open and looking into the room, we saw that she was lying on the floor. She was in the habit of having a nap in the afternoon, and I thought she might have fainted and fallen off the sofa. When we got to her, however, we found that she was cold, and at once saw that there had been foul play. The cushion from the couch was tied tightly over her face with a piece of gauze or string which went right round her neck and the knot was so tight that we could not release it. Her hands were tied together with a pocket handkerchief and were across her breast. My wife tried to get the cushion off her face while I at once went for Dr Fraser, who lives a few doors down.

He came back to the shop with me and found that she was dead. There was a wound on the left side of her head, by the ear, as though she had been struck by some instrument, and the blood had trickled down over her face. Her purse was on the table, cut open. It had been emptied. This was the purse she wore under her dress. By the purse lay an ordinary table knife, which had evidently been used for cutting it open. There was also some bread and cheese on the table. We went upstairs to see if anything was missing, and found that her room had been ransacked. Some of the boxes were lying open, but there were one or two locked which had not been forced.

Superintendent John Pearman was in charge of Slough's police force, and he arrived at the crime scene shortly afterwards. The premises were searched and constables sent throughout the town to try and apprehend the culprit. Bloodstained rags were found in the fireplace. These may have been rags that the killer had wiped his hands on and then tried to destroy.

The following day, Pearman called Major Otway Mayne, Chief Constable of the county, and they met with three officers from Scotland Yard; Chief Inspector Bower, Inspector Munro and Detective Sergeant Burton.

Clearly, the motive for the crime was theft. Death had occurred in the afternoon (the corpse was cold when the doctor had arrived), and the deceased's skull had been fractured. Marks on her hands were due to an attempt to shield herself from the killer's blows. She had been knocked unconscious by blows to her face, possibly caused by a heavy instrument such as a burglar's jemmy. She died, however, from suffocation caused by the cushion being placed over her face. Inspector Munro of the fingerprint department brushed the shop for clues, but the only prints he found were smudged and so of no use. No weapon was found.

Initially, there was a rumour that a couple had been trying to change money in a Slough pub on the night of the murder. These people were soon traced to Windsor and were brought into Slough police station, but were able, however, to give a good account of themselves and were released without charge.

In any case, the focus of the investigation took a more promising turn on the day after the murder. Witnesses approached the police to tell them that a suspicious character had been seen in the vicinity at the time of the murder – William Brooks, a twenty-six-year-old former soldier. He was the son of the late manager of the shop next door to Mrs Wilson's. His family had left Slough in June 1910. It was known that Brooks was in the Berkshire Yeomanry and had served as a regular in the Northamptonshire Regiment during the Boer War.

Brooks was arrested in Harlesden, London, at 5.45 p.m. on Sunday 17 July. He had two parallel scratches on his right cheek. Chief Inspector Bower met him outside the police station and stated, 'I am a police officer. I believe your name is William Broome?'

'Brooks,' came the reply.

'Well, you are the man I want to see. A very serious thing has happened and it is necessary that I should ask you to give me an account of your movements during the past three or four days,' continued Bower.

'I've done nothing.'

'If you don't mind, we will go into the police station and write down what you say.'

Brooks went with Bower into the police station and his lengthy statement was taken down by Detective Sergeant Burton. Brooks explained that he had enlisted in the 2nd battalion of the Northamptonshire Regiment for a term of seven years. He had served in the Boer War, where he had been awarded two medals. The remainder of his service had taken place in India, in the 1st battalion. He was discharged with a good character reference in December 1907. He then lived with his parents at 34 Albert Street, Oxford Road, Reading, where his father managed a shop for Singer's Sewing Machine Company.

Since about March 1910 he had been living in lodgings in London, firstly on 38 York Road, then at 104 Albert Street. He moved to a room in the Lexius family's house at 146 Albany Street on 12 July.

On Thursday 14 July he rose at about nine o'clock. He then had breakfast in a café on Villiers Street, The Strand. He then went to Holborn Library and read job adverts in the newspapers there. Leaving at 11.30 a.m., he met a friend, whose name and address he did not know, on York Road, Lambeth. By the evening he was in Hyde Park, listening to the speakers. He met an acquaintance from Holborn there – again, he did not know his name or address. At ten o'clock he returned to Albany Street and went to bed.

On the day of the murder – Friday – Brooks stated that he rose at half past eight. After washing and shaving, he went again to the same eating place at Villiers Street. He then went to the carriage department at Scotland Yard and handed in an application form for registration as a cab driver (Scotland Yard administered the granting of hansom cab licences at this time). At 10.20 a.m., Brooks was told that all forms had to be handed in by ten. He was too late. Brooks then went to The Trafalgar pub in St Martin's Lane. For three pence he lunched on bread, cheese and drank stout. Returning to his lodgings, he recalled seeing a servant there at half past one. He read a newspaper and messed about, before leaving an hour later. He walked to a grocer's shop near Cambridge Terrace and bought a postcard. He wrote it to Ellen Bunce and posted it at three o'clock. The message read: 'Dear Ellen, Will be at Tube tomorrow Saturday 11 p.m. Can't see you tonight.'

Brooks then went to Hyde Park, arriving at four. He met a friend there, whose name began with a P, but was otherwise unidentifiable. He left for home between five and six. He saw his landlady there. Between 6 and 7.30 p.m. he was in his room, reading, and then he washed and went to The Britannia public house in Camden Town. At 10.30 p.m. he returned home, after seeing no one, and went to bed.

On Saturday morning he again rose at 8.30 a.m. He went to The Britannia pub and met a man about some bets, and stayed and talked to him for a while. He went to have breakfast at William Street, then to the public carriage department at Scotland Yard again. He took the exam for a licence to drive a taxi, but failed and was informed that he would have to wait another two weeks before he could re-sit it.

The next day he had breakfast in bed, and left his lodgings at 11 a.m. He went to his father's house at 4 Drayton Road, Harlesden, and was taken up by the police shortly afterwards. Brooks stressed, 'I was not down at Slough last week at any time,' before stating:

> The scratches I have on my right cheek were done last Saturday by the man I had a few words with outside The Britannia public house, Camden Town. It was a blow given to me during the scuffle and my eye has been discoloured. The man who did it employs a man whom I know by the name of 'Ginger' to collect bets for him around the lavatory outside The Britannia.

Brooks described the man as being over forty, 5ft 6in tall, with a dark moustache, stout, wearing a black bowler hat and a brown jacket. Brooks said he did not know where he lived. He added, 'I hit him in the stomach but did not mark him as far as I know.' It will be noted that very little in his statement could be

Camden Town.

corroborated. None of the men he spoke to, nor the one who caused his injuries, could be identified, or confirm his story or disprove it.

Brooks' lodgings at 146 Albany Street, Regent's Park, were searched by DS Burch, and, oddly for a man reputed to be in poverty, nineteen sovereigns and two half sovereigns were found in a portmanteau. He also found a pair of old boots, stained with a removal agent.

Brooks was examined by Dr Alexander Carson Smythe, who said that the two marks on his right cheek, which were probably caused by fingernails, had been acquired two or three days previously, though Brooks had said they were caused by buttons on his coat. He was charged with murder, to which he replied, 'Of course you can charge me with what you like. I cannot help that. Me? Commit murder? I would not kill a fly!' Brooks was sent to Slough police station the following day, and was soon brought before the local magistrates, where numerous witnesses gathered evidence against him.

Meanwhile, on Thursday 20 July, Mrs Wilson was buried in the parish churchyard in the same grave as her husband and her mother-in-law, near to the south gate of the churchyard. There was great sympathy among the town for her and subsequently a large attendance at her funeral. Despite a minimum of publicity, many people gathered outside her home when the cortege left at quarter past three that afternoon. After playing the Death March, the procession proceeded down Windsor Road and along Albert Street to the baptist church. Reverend Theo Cousens conducted a most impressive service, after Mr Luke's beautiful solo on the organ, 'O Rest in the Lord'. There were three floral tributes. One from William and Elisabeth, her nephew and niece, one from Alice and Albert, and one from Mr Hammerslag, an old friend. Due to the crowds, Superintendent Pearman and twenty-five policemen were on duty, but there were no scenes of disorder, the crowds being most reverent in their behaviour.

On 20 July, Brooks was charged with the murder at Slough Magistrates' Court. His defence counsel, Mr Pierron, said that Brooks strongly denied the charge, but that he realised that the police had a case to complete and so would not oppose their application that his client be remanded for a week. Brooks was then sent to Reading Prison.

At the inquest, the Whites gave their evidence regarding the discovery of the body, Ellen Bunce of Chalk Farm, London, employed as a theatre attendant in Hampstead, was questioned about her relationship with Brooks. She had known him for three years – since he had lived in Reading. They had been to a music hall together and had taken a walk, and visited London together on two occasions. Their friendship had deepened in January 1910 when they had begun to live together, firstly in Glen House, York Road, near Waterloo. Although Brooks had been in work as a motor driver and earned between 15s and £1, she often had to pay their rent, food bills and supply him with cigarette money. There was talk of marriage, but he appeared to lack prospects and they ceased living together on 10 July. Yet the parting was amicable, as he carried her belongings to her new lodgings. She confirmed that they had met on 14 July and 16 July, but not on the intervening day.

It is perhaps of note to learn that Brooks had sent a postcard to his mother on the Saturday after the murder. It read: 'Dear Mother, May be home tomorrow. Have been busy. Have you read that about poor old Mrs Wilson? – William.'

A week later, Ryland Adkins, representing the Director of Public Prosecutions, outlined the case against Brooks. Adkins stated that Brooks had been seen in the vicinity of the deceased's shop in central Slough, between half past twelve and three on the day on the murder, by George Dollar of Rose Villas, Springfield Road, who worked for the Slough and District Electricity Company. He knew Brooks well, having been a neighbour of his. Mr Dollar stated, 'He came down the White Hart Yard and went in the direction of where he used to live.' Edward Roe, a newsagent on William Street, also remembered seeing Brooks on that day, between twelve and one. He had seen him walking towards the High Street. PC Harding also saw Brooks, at about half past twelve on the corner of McKenzie Street and the High Street, smoking a cigarette.

He had also been seen by Mrs Pearson, wife of the publican of The Western pub in William Street, Slough. She recalled him entering the bar at 12.40. She said:

> I saw sitting in the chair a young man whom I recognised as William Brooks. He was sitting just inside the door leading from the private room. He had in front of him a bottle and a glass. He also had the *Daily Mail* in his hand. There was no one else in the bar at the time.

She had known Brooks by sight for some months and also recalled that his face was unmarked. Thomas Pearson remembered that he gave his wife three pence for beer on that occasion. They had talked about horse racing, before Brooks left at one o'clock.

Once in London, Brooks was seen at Messrs Allen Ltd, a chemist's shop at 155 Praed Street, at around three o'clock asking for a preparation to remove scratch marks from his face. Axell Auderberg, the assistant there, asked, 'Have you been fighting?' Brook replied, 'Oh, its nothing much.' Auderberg then said, 'It looks as if you had been fighting with a woman.' Brooks said that he had been hit by the wing of a motorcar and wanted it as least noticeable as possible. Auderberg then dressed his face with boric hazel and witch hazel, and thought his manner was rather strange, though when asked in court to pick out Brooks, he said, 'I could not positively swear to him, having only seen him for about seven to ten minutes.'

Two hours later, Brooks had been at a similar shop in Oxford Street, owned by Evan Albert Idris Phillips, making similar enquiries. Phillips showed an entry made in his shop's records to the effect that a bottle of lotion and a packet of cotton wool had been bought from him on 15 July, and that he sold them to Brooks.

It did seem that the scratches had been inflicted on 15 July, for Anna Lexius, with whom Brooks lodged, recalled that she had spoken to him at 5 p.m. that day and remembered the marks. According to her, Brooks said that people might think on seeing them that he had robbed someone. Mrs Lexius had replied, 'Oh, nobody would think that,' to which Brook replied, 'Oh, many people would.' He then said he had had an accident resulting in these injuries.

Albert Tuersley, a boot shop owner in Tottenham Court Road, recalled that between 4.15 and 4.45 p.m. he had sold new boots to Brooks for 10s 6d – indicative that Brooks had more money than earlier, and that he was hastily in need of new footwear.

Two witnesses also questioned the alleged fight outside The Britannia pub. Arthur Butler of Arlington Road, Camden Town, a timekeeper employed by the Camden Town Omnibus Association, worked at 158 Camden Town High Street, opposite the pub, and did not recall any disturbance on the evening of 16 July, nor did he know a man by the name of 'Ginger'. A colleague, Henry Johnson, agreed with this statement.

At the next hearing, Mr Pierron cross-examined the witnesses for the prosecution. He wanted to show that Brooks had had sufficient funds prior to the murder. Ellen Bunce stated that on Thursday 14 July, Brooks had treated her to a place of amusement, paid for both their teas and suppers, and then paid her travel fares. She thought that this money was Brook's camp money – the amount paid to him, as an army reservist, whilst he had last been on a training camp.

However, there was evidence that Brooks needed money; in fact he had written to Messrs Alan and Dawes of Norwich on four occasions between 2 and 16 July, offering them a broach for sale. Initially he had asked for £6, before dropping his asking price to £2 10s. He had also written to ask for his army reserve pay.

Since 10 December 1907, when he left the army, he had been in the reserves, and was granted sixpence per day, which was paid in quarterly sums of £2 5s 6d. He should have received it on 1 July, but he had not updated the paymaster of his new address and it had been sent to the Slough address instead. He then wrote to tell them that it should be sent to his parents' address in Harlesden. On 12 July, having still not received it, he wrote, 'I am still without news as to my last quarter's reserve pay. Can you please tell me the cause of delay? It is now ten days overdue and has put me to no end of inconvenience.' Brooks was clearly in need of cash, since he was unemployed. He even pawned goods, only to retrieve them on the day after the murder. Henry Bright stated that Brooks' two young sisters were often at Mrs Wilson's shop. He may well have known that she had money on her person.

As said, Brooks was unemployed and was trying to obtain employment as a taxi driver. Miss Clara Sant, assistant secretary of the Motor Drivers' Union, first saw Brooks on 9 February 1910. He had given his name as William Brooks, 34 Howard Street, Reading, single and aged twenty-four. He paid a fee of four guineas for the driver training course provided by the Union. He had passed on 19 March, by which time he was living at 38 York Road.

Dr Willcox, senior scientific analyst to the Home Office, and who had recently been involved in the notorious case of Dr Crippen, also gave evidence. He had been given Brooks' boots and collar on 21 July. The former had bloodstains on them, and the latter was brownish in colour, as if blood had been washed off recently. He had also examined the fingernails on the dead woman's hands and concluded that they had drawn blood from her attacker. On the brown paper found at the crime scene he found seventeen minute particles of gold – marks of what had been coins, and gold sovereigns.

The prosecution was concluded on 12 August. It was as follows: Brooks had very little money before the murder, but shortly afterwards was in funds. He was uninjured before the day of the murder, but was injured afterwards – and it was known that Mrs Wilson had scratched her attacker. He lied about not having been in Slough at the time of the murder. Brooks pleaded not guilty; however, he reserved his defence and was committed for trial at the Aylesbury Assizes.

Over two months later, on 23 October, Brooks stood trial and pleaded not guilty. Mr Poyser defended him, instructed by Mr S.E. Wilkins of Aylesbury. Although Brooks stepped lightly into the dock, he took a keen interest in the proceedings as the case for the prosecution was made, followed by the statements of the witnesses for the Crown. He made notes during this time, which he passed to Poyser, and when Miss Bunce gave her evidence he was noticeably snarling at his former lover.

He then gave a fresh account of his movements on 15 July: 'After having been at Scotland Yard, I then made my way to Paddington Station. I went by the longest way – Tottenham Court Road – by the bus.' He then said that he alighted at the junction of Hampstead and Euston Road, telling the court that he went there on purpose 'to see a fellow – a bookmaker – who owed me some money. I saw him and spoke to him. There was a little difference between us over the amount . . . and there was a bit of a scuffle, not a fight. He scratched my face and made marks upon it.' He then caught another bus to Paddington and took a train from there to Windsor, arriving at about noon. This was so he could visit the Yeomanry barracks, despite having been discharged on 19 May, but could find no one there.

He then went to Slough and visited The Western pub, before walking up William Street. He recalled seeing Mr Roe, whom he talked to, before walking along the High Street. In all, he had only spent about half an hour in Slough. He then returned to London – leaving Paddington at two o'clock. He then went to the chemists on Praed Street. Later he bought a postcard and sent it, then went to Tottenham Court Road to buy new boots at a shop there. He denied committing the murder or having any contact with Mrs Wilson.

When cross-examined about the differences in his story, as he had earlier denied having been in Slough, he claimed that he had been drunk when he made his initial statement and did not know what he was signing – he now claimed that it was entirely inaccurate. He added that he had lied to the police because he did not want to be suspected of the crime, and added, 'It is not a nice thing to tell anyone that you've been fighting.' The jury, however, found him guilty and Justice Buckmill sentenced him to death. He was escorted back to Reading on the train, and on arrival saw some familiar faces among the crowd, to whom he smiled.

However, due to the recent innovation of the Court of Appeal (established in 1907), there was one last hope for Brooks. Mr Attenborough appeared for Brooks on 7 November, and Adkins represented the Crown, as he had done previously. Attenborough stated the basic facts of the crime. He then argued that the evidence against Brooks was purely circumstantial. According to him, it was unlikely that Mrs Wilson would have had such a sum on her person as her clients would have been too poor to pay such sums, and that the money in Brooks possession had come to him as a result of his work as a dealer, and that he could bring Brooks' mother to testify to her son being in funds prior to the murder. He also said that the judge's summing up was improper because he had not told the jury that the evidence against Brooks was faulty. Furthermore, Brooks had a good character and was not in need of money, so was clearly innocent. Attenborough concluded by arguing that the motor-cyclist seen by the Whites outside the shop on the day of the murder or a passing tramp had committed the crime. The defence's case was dismissed.

Brooks was hanged at Reading Prison at eight o'clock on the morning of Thursday 24 November. His executioner was John Ellis, who had hanged the infamous Dr Crippen on the previous day. Brooks had been to bed at the usual time on the previous night, slept fairly well and had had a substantial breakfast. He did not make a confession, but retained the cold demeanour that he had shown since his arrest. Unlike Mrs Wilson, his death was instantaneous, with a six-and-a-half foot drop following an unaided walk to the scaffold. About a dozen people waited outside the gaol for the posting of the notice on the gates.

There seems little doubt that Brooks was indeed guilty. He had the opportunity, means and motive. He needed money and he knew of a defenceless target, known to have a reasonable sum of money on her person. He travelled down to Slough from London and assaulted the woman, who put up a fight before being overpowered and robbed of her money. Brooks' attempts to cover his tracks by changing stories only sealed his guilt.

Superintendent Pearman was specially commended by the judge at the trial, for his successful endeavour in bringing the guilty man to justice.

11

AN ETON MURDER

Eton, 1912

Mention Eton to almost anyone and they will instantly think of the world-famous boys' public school near Windsor, founded by Henry VI in 1440. It has educated many who went on to gain prominence in later life; prime ministers, generals, authors and others. Prince William, David Cameron and Boris Johnson are among its famous alumni. Any novel or work of fiction dealing with skulduggery at the school is almost certain to dwell upon the masters and pupils, especially those with famous connections.

The Sunday afternoon of 24 November 1912 turned out to be anything but restful and tranquil. Boys were seen running along Eton Wick Road to the police station on the High Street. The cause of this disturbance had taken place at Cotton Hall House on that very road. This house was one of about twenty-four houses in which the schoolboys of Eton College boarded; about forty to a house. It had been built in 1869-1870 when the college's numbers were rising. It was run by a college assistant master, Mr Robert Pearson Lee Booker, MA, FSA, a Classics master.

Inspector George Marks, in charge of the Eton police, and PC More went to Cotton Hall House, arriving at about half past four. They met servant Eric James Sedgwick in the servants' hall. He gave the Inspector a knife and a newspaper. The knife had a slightly curved blade, on which there was a bloodstain. Looking into the the servants' hall, Marks saw the body of a young woman in a wicker chair. Her clothing was slightly undone, but ominously there was a wound just below her left breast. With her were two female servants, including Ethel Waugh.

Sedgwick was taken to another room, where he gave his name, occupation and address. He then gave a brief explanation: 'The girl, Annie, who is lying in the chair, I have been keeping company with for three years.' Inspector Marks went back next door, where he was informed that the woman was dead. He returned to Sedgwick to tell him this news, and cautioned him. Sedgwick asked, 'Is she dead?' Marks replied, 'Yes, and you will be charged with wilfully murdering her.' Sedgwick made no response. He was searched, and in his pockets a knife sheath and a bloodstained handkerchief were found. He was then led from the scene, saying, 'It would have been better had we parted than this.'

Sedgwick was taken to Slough police station by cab. During the journey he muttered, 'They have parted us now.' At the police station, Superintendent Pearman took over and charged him with the murder, to which he made no reply. It was noted that he had bloodstained fingers, which he put to his mouth, uttering the words, 'Poor girl,' before kissing them. Inspector Marks returned to Eton and had the corpse transferred to the mortuary, which was behind the fire station. He noticed that there were two cuts in her clothing, where the knife had penetrated.

The former Eton police station on the High Street.

Dr Wilfred Henry Waller Attlee of 25 High Street, Eton, conducted a post-mortem. He found that the stab wound was an inch-and-a-quarter deep, and was between the ribs. Death was due to bleeding, and that much force would have been needed to kill her. Unless anyone with medical knowledge had been on the scene at the time of the attack, there was nothing that anyone could have done to save her life.

The following day, PC More went to Sedgwick's late place of employment – the National Liberal Club – where he searched Sedgwick's belongings. On a shelf in the cupboard, he found an envelope on which was written, 'Not to be opened unless something serious happens to me – Eric'. Inside the envelope was a sheet of paper bearing the following message:

> To whoever may open this – In the event of my death, by whatever cause, I wish everything I possess to be given to my sweetheart, with the undermentioned exceptions . . . Trusting that she will never forget that I have always placed her first in my love and estimation.

Not everything was to go to Annie, though the other woman to whom bequests were made was never mentioned in the press. The note also read, 'This momento [a portrait of a dog and one of himself] she has earned by her great kind-heartedness, and thought for my sweetheart and myself.'

The story behind this crime began to unfold at the inquest, which was held at Eton Fire Station on Tuesday 26 November, before Mr A.E.W. Chareley, the coroner for South Buckinghamshire.

Sedgwick had been taken by car from Slough police station, handcuffed to PS George Kirby. As was the case at the time, the jury had the task of viewing the corpse before proceedings could begin.

Frederick Anthony Davis of Blenheim Stables, Streatham, was the first to give evidence. He was the brother of the deceased and he confirmed the dead woman's identity. He stated that she had turned twenty-two on her last birthday, that she was single and had worked at Cotton Hall House since 26 August 1912. He knew she had been seeing Sedgwick, though he knew little of the man himself, only knowing him as Eric. He stated that their parents were still alive, living at Glass House Green, Wentworth, near to Rotherham in Yorkshire, and that he did not think they objected to the two as a couple.

Most of the evidence of the events leading up to the murder was given by Edith Alice Armstrong, head housemaid at Cotton Hall House, who said she had known Annie since 1908, when she began her employment there. According

Eton Fire Station.

to Edith, Annie and Sedgwick had been acquainted since January 1910, and he had visited her in Eton on several occasions. She told the inquest that, 'They seemed on friendly terms.' On one occasion, Annie had told her that Sedgwick had given her a lot of trouble and she seemed very much upset after she had seen him several times. Edith believed that, 'She seemed to be frightened of him . . . He had threatened her before he came to Eton. He threatened to do for her in front of her mother.'

Edith then detailed the pair's meetings. She recalled that Sedgwick first came to Eton on Saturday 5 October, and that the two spent the evening together, with Annie returning at a quarter to ten. She was much troubled and was in tears. Apparently, there were difficulties between Sedgwick and Annie's parents, but she did not specify what these were. Sedgwick was staying at The Three Lillies Coffee Tavern and saw her again on Sunday morning. Annie returned to Cotton Hall House at 12.45 that afternoon, in a better frame of mind. Likewise, when they met later that day she was in much higher spirits. The couple met again on Monday afternoon and had tea, before going to the theatre. Sedgwick remained in Eton until Friday, continuing to spend time with Annie. On the penultimate day of his visit, Annie became upset when Sedgwick told her that he was going to Kempton Park, against her wishes. He went anyway, leaving the keys to his luggage with Annie.

Sedgwick's next visit to Eton was on Wednesday 16 October. He sent Annie a telegram prior to his visit, but she was unable to meet him because that day was Edith's day off, not hers. At quarter past eight that evening, Sedgwick called at the back door of Cotton Hall House and asked Annie for the keys he had left. He snatched them out of her hand and then left. Naturally, Annie was very upset. She later received a letter of apology from Sedgwick, who blamed his actions on his beastly temper.

The two next met on Sunday 10 November, at Eton railway station. They had afternoon tea and seemed on friendly terms. They spent the evening together and said their farewells at the railway station. On her return to Cotton Hall House, Edith thought that Annie seemed well, but was rather quiet. On the following day, she told Edith that, 'Eric told me a dreadful secret which will worry me to the grave.' She did not enlighten Edith as to what the secret was.

Eton, c. 1900s.

Sedgwick was to have come down on either the 13th or 20th of November, but did not do so because Annie wrote to him telling him it was not her day off. So, he arrived on the Sunday afternoon of 24 November; the scene was set for tragedy.

Sedgwick arrived at Cotton Hall House between 3.30 and 4 p.m. He said to Edith, 'Good afternoon, I hope you are well,' before shaking hands with her and being invited into the servants' hall. Annie had been lying on her bed, resting, and, on being told that Eric had come to visit her, she replied, 'Oh no, he has not.' She then turned deathly pale. Edith said to her, 'I wish you wouldn't go and see him,' but Annie answered, 'I must. You go down first. I shake like an aspen leaf.' Sedgwick and Annie met in a room adjacent to the servants' hall, where Edith left them alone. Annie was standing by the fireplace and told Sedgwick, 'You will have to go now.'

Edith warned Annie Saunders, a kitchen maid, to be on the alert whilst she went upstairs. Here, she met Mrs Booker, the master's wife, and a servant, who she asked to come downstairs with her. On doing so, they saw a terrible sight. Edith recalled that, 'Blood was flowing from Annie's side, but her clothes were not damaged.' She saw Sedgwick nearby and said, 'Oh, Eric, Eric, what have you done? You have killed her.' Sedgwick replied, 'For God's sake, Edith, bring some water.' She did so, and Sedgwick tried to pour water down Annie's throat. Sedgwick kept muttering, 'She is not dead. She is not dead,' before saying, 'Annie, speak to me, speak to me. They will not part us.' He kept kissing her, and added mysteriously, 'You are not a Davis.' Turning to his audience, he implored, 'For God's sake, can't somebody stop this bleeding?'

Ethel Waugh, a servant, told Sedgwick to move aside whilst she loosened Annie's clothing. Mr Annesley Ashworth Somerville, MA, master of the adjacent hall, arrived on the scene and took Sedgwick to the room next door. Dr Attlee arrived then, but he was too late. Annie was dead.

Evidence was taken from Inspector Marks, PC More and Dr Attlee. The latter was asked whether this could have been a case of suicide and he replied that it was possible. The jury though, having heard all the evidence to date, decided that this was a case of murder and that Sedgwick was responsible. Sedgwick responded to the news in a calm manner.

The hearing was held at the Magistrates' Court at Slough on the Monday and Wednesday following the murder. A description of the accused man was also provided. Apparently, he was a man of sallow complexion, clean shaven and average height, he appeared cool and collected. He wore a heavy winter coat, a red waistcoat and brown boots covered by spats; he was aged twenty-seven. Sedgwick was remanded until the next hearing the following week. He asked

Dr Attlee's house, Eton high street.

if he could smoke whilst in custody and was told he could not, but this ban was eventually revoked on medical grounds.

When the hearing was resumed, on 4 December, more evidence was heard. It was learnt that Sedgwick spent seven years in the Durham Light Infantry, part of which he had served in India. He had been discharged in February 1910. He had been on intimate terms with Annie and marriage had been talked of. This information was garnered from a number of letters which had been found, both to and from Sedgwick, and shed much light on the immediate background to the murder. A letter, written by Sedgwick on 21 October, reveals his character and his feelings for Annie. He wrote:

Sweetheart, my dearest,
Now girlie, to write to you the letter I promised you yesterday. I went to this 'Vic' last night. It was very good. There were one or two turns you would have enjoyed especially. It will be such a treat to take you some time, deary. You shall have a treat one of these days. I was so glad to get your letter the other day. I thought

that as I had been such a pig you would not want ever to see me again. You dear little creature, I was so glad you could forgive me that nasty temper of mine again. Coming down on the train I whistled all the way. Oh! I was disappointed. I came back bad tempered. I wrote a postcard to mother [Annie's mother], but what I put on it I don't exactly remember. I had very little sleep and I thought of our week and if I found fault then, my love, for you made me look over it.

Yes dear, you have done what you can for me; there is nothing I would not do for you. I remembered you only as you were that night on the 16th, and I wanted you again to kiss as you did and say it was only me you wanted. I could not part with you; I want you with me now. Promise me, sweetheart, that you will come to me for good. It makes me dissatisfied with everything if you are not there. I want you and it makes me sigh even when I go for a walk because you are not with me. In the performance last night I was thinking of our week (I was in the gallery) and it made me wish for you more and more, and I made up my mind that it won't be long before I have you up here (if you have thoroughly forgiven me) for always. Everything is so different. I like this place (the city, I mean) and so will you. The week after this, you must come up for a day.

It is my Sunday out today, but later on I will get it changed to the same Sundays as yours, then who knows, but what we might not have a day, or you would get a weekend and come up here. I would put a pass in, and we would have our old times over again, times when there were not two happier persons in the world, than we two.

I've always tried to make you happy, and there is nothing gives me greater pleasure, as it makes me real down miserable when we have these tiffs. Oh Annie, what do they mean? Is it the beginning of a separation, or what? Do you really love me as much as you did then? Or have you seen someone who has made you wish you have never seen me.

Since I left Burswell things have seemed so different, perhaps it is in me, perhaps I am impatient, or I have gone and let my temper get the best of me when I should not have done. Anyway, let us drop it. I've sometimes found fault when perhaps I ought not to have done, but let us forget dearest. They make me miserable. I could not bear many more of them, so let us try and avoid them somehow. I shall not come down this week, girlie.

I am on weekly payments now, and I haven't got very much at present. This job is no good for me, except only in one way, and that is I am learning my way about a bit. I shall have to learn the streets and learn to save some money before they have me as a driver anywhere. I think if I stop here during the New Year I should have enough knowledge by then to try and make a bit of money. By the time you come up here I will be able to show you around the shops and try and give you a good time. You needn't get up here before 4.30, but you will want to get extra time for night, unless you get some for Saturday night and a whole day on Sunday. Say you were stopping at Fred's.

You will open your eyes a bit when I show you some of the things I have found out since I came here. There are fellows out of here on 9s a week. You won't see their underclothes, but you would think they had nothing less than £5 a week. Well, you would really think that their fathers are great shareholders. How do they do it?

Sweetheart, you want to break it gently to them that you might stay only there until February. Drop it in gradually, and then if I cannot get you away at Christmas, they will ask ridiculous questions. Unless you see a likely place up here, but do not try for a place in a big club or a hotel; make sure of a private family. If Mrs B says anything about your leaving, say I fell out of work and it is not so suitable at present to get moved on.

Write to me soon, girlie. What days are to be your days out? Let me know dearest. There ought to be trips on your days. I just about have every evening. Ta, ta. I care for you just the same, girlie, as I did on our week. It bound us together. From your loving Eric.

P.S. If you change, Annie, no one shall have you. I'll take care, and tell me, sweetheart, if my dear own is in all ways improving. I am still anxious.

Shortly afterwards, Annie wrote a letter back, which contained the following ominous sentence, 'In this world, necessity, stern driver, drives sternly. A warm welcome attends murderer's exit.'

A letter from Sedgwick to his mother also refers to Annie thus:

Tonight I went down whistling and came back cursing. Why? Because there is something about Annie. I waited two hours for her, so as to keep away from the house, but she never turned out. Said to herself, I expect, 'Oh he knows where I live. He'll turn out alright.' I did, and I shall be turning up one of these nights, and I'll see she doesn't leave me.

Then there was a letter from Annie, sent on 24 November but never received by Sedgwick. It reveals her current feelings for Sedgwick, which were presumably made clear to him on that fatal afternoon:

Eric,

I am writing a few lines to tell you, that you and I must part at once, forever.

I have found out you are not the man for me, for you have been unfaithful to me in everything. I have found out and I see through it to my sorrow.

I am sorry I have sinned as I did through you, and sinned through you because I loved you. It was you who made me sin, and I see now we shall only go on sinning. So to prevent it I must part from you. I ought never to have stuck to you after 'our week' but I have, just because I gave myself to you.

I feel I can never face another man. I can see you did not do it for love, while you will do the same to any woman. God has shown me you are not a good man, but I am doing this for the best of both of us. I have confessed all here and also to mother, and now I am going to lead a straight life and a pure one. I cannot keep what we have done any longer, for it was driving me silly. To get all out of my mind is a happy release. Do not come here on Wednesday, for I cannot see you again. If you come I will refuse to see you, for I do not want to see you again. Forget you ever saw me, and I must do the same, and so good night forever, goodbye.

Annie.

It is not certain what lies behind Annie's wanting to end the affair with Sedgwick, but it is possible that there might have been some religious influence, and the use of the word 'confession' suggests Catholicism. It also suggests that the two had had intimate relations.

Emily Jane Mills, a parlour maid at Cotton Hall House, recalled that at 3.30 on the afternoon of the murder, the doorbell rang and later, at ten past four, she heard a scuffle and a scream. When she first saw the dying Annie, she also saw Sedgwick standing over her, and thought he was strangling her. She shouted at Sedgwick to leave her colleague alone. Charles Sear, a hall porter at the National Liberal Club, who shared the same bedroom as Sedgwick, recalled having seen the murder weapon before in Sedgwick's possession. Apparently he had brought the knife home as a souvenir of his time in India.

Dr Attlee was also called upon to give evidence. He said that it was probable that Annie was not a virgin. Sedgwick then demanded that he state that Annie was not diseased in any way, and the doctor confirmed this was the case. Sedgwick also contradicted PC More's evidence about where he had located his letters – PC More alleged that he had found them in Sedgwick's cupboard at the club, but this was denied.

Sedgwick was committed to the next assizes, charged with wilfully murdering Annie Davis, to which Sedgwick said, 'Wilfully, no.' He showed far more emotion now than he had done before.

In the meantime, a train took Annie's body to her parents' home in Yorkshire. Brooker and some of Annie's fellow servants laid floral tributes to her on top of the coffin. The funeral was held at Holy Trinity Church, Wentworth, and was conducted by Revd Remington Jones. There was a large turn out, despite snow being six inches deep on the ground. The coffin had the simple inscription: 'Annie Wentworth Davis, died November 24th 1912, aged 22 years'.

The trial took place at the Buckinghamshire Assizes at Aylesbury on Wednesday, 15 January 1913. Sedgwick was smartly dressed, and in a strong voice announced that he was 'Not Guilty.' The prosecution called upon Edith Armstrong as the chief witness, as well as Dr Attlee and Inspector Marks. The defence was in the hands of Mr Campian. He stated that Sedgwick was in love with Annie, as shown by his bringing chocolate and flowers to her on the day of her death. He said that there was no evidence of any quarrel, and, indeed, there were no witnesses to the fatal act itself. He argued that Sedgwick was a highly strung character and had acted under a dreadful impulsive insanity, having become suddenly mentally imbalanced. He also pointed out that Sedgwick had made no attempt to escape afterwards. There was no real doubt that Annie had been murdered and that Sedgwick had killed her, and it was deemed unnecessary for the prosecution to prove a motive. The jury took just ten minutes to decide their verdict and found Sedgwick guilty of murder. Unusually, however, after the judge had asked the condemned man if he had anything to say, Sedgwick made quite a speech. He said, 'There was never any intention on my part to kill my sweetheart. I am responsible for her death . . . I deny that such a thing as a quarrel ever took place between us, no jealousy, no lust.' Then, in a deliberate riposte to the judge's concluding remark – 'And may God have mercy on your soul' – he said, 'May the Lord have mercy on the people who have brought me to this.'

Curiously enough, the same assizes had resulted in another man being found guilty of murdering his sweetheart, too. Philip Trueman had killed Dora Hussey in Bourne End that autumn. However, he was reprieved and sentenced to penal servitude for life, which meant imprisonment with hard labour. Sedgwick was not reprieved. Before his death he wrote the following letter to the prison governor:

Dear Sir,

Before I take leave of you in this world, I wish to state that the statement I made at my trial was the truth. Circumstances of which no explanation has been given brought about a momentary lapse, in which I caused the death of that person most dear to me. Passionately fond of my sweetheart, with her died all my hopes in this world, and I have no desire to live. My death satisfies the laws of this country, and, willingly given, may be some atonement in the sight of God. I desire to thank you and all other officials who have had me in their charge for the kindness extended to me during my stay in the prison.

To the end I remain,

Obediently yours,

Eric James Sedgwick

Sedgwick was executed at Reading Prison on Tuesday, 4 February 1913.

It seems that Sedgwick had two lovers, and that Annie had learnt about the existence of the other. She had already given herself to him sexually, probably believing he was true to her. The revelation of the other woman led her to break off relations with him. However, he was intensely in love with her and would brook no refusal. He had no idea that she wanted to stop seeing him, so when he arrived at Cotton Hall House on that fatal Sunday afternoon, he was shocked; more than shocked. His mental upset led to violence. This was presumably not premeditated, but, on the other hand, he did have a knife on his person, though whether he ordinarily carried it for self-defence or out of habit, we do not know.

12

A DOUBLE MURDER

Little Kimble, 1914

Just as the First World War got underway, a small village in Buckinghamshire found itself the scene of a more domestic slaughter. PC Joseph Dillow and Herbert Howard, stationmaster, both of Little Kimble, had a rude start to their day on Saturday, 29 August 1914. At 7.35 a.m. they were directed to the tool shed by the railway station, which was, normally, a repository for the tools used by the men who worked on the railway line. In the shed they found the bodies of two men, Charles Busby and Walter Tucker, platelayers who worked on the line. It was suggested that the men had been murdered by a mysterious stranger, who had attacked a signalman at Northchurch, earlier on. The truth was more mundane, though no less horrifying.

To understand the murder, we need to go back to the previous year. Thomas Gilbert and his family lived at 3 Icknield Cottages, Little Kimble, from April 1913. He was a foreman platelayer for the Great Western and Great Central Railway, and was then aged forty-five. He had been born in Blidworth, Nottinghamshire and in 1911 lived in East Kirby with his wife, Letty, and their three daughters, aged between twelve and sixteen.

Since autumn 1913, there were two platelayers working under his command. These were Charles Thomas Busby, aged twenty-nine, who lived at Thame Road, Princes Risborough, and Walter Tucker, aged twenty-six, of Owlswick. Both men were unmarried, though Tucker was engaged to a Miss Webb. Busby had been born in Battersea in 1885, but by 1891 was living with his family in Princes Risborough. By 1911 he was a railway employee. In 1913, the three

Platform at Little Kimble railway station.

men had worked on a section of the railway between Little Kimble and Marsh Crossing. However, all was not well between them.

In October 1913, Tucker complained to his uncle that Gilbert was not a good foreman to work under, but did not explain why and had not made any similar remarks subsequently. Up to 26 August 1914, Albert Edward Stone, another platelayer, also worked with them. On the 13th, Gilbert had taken him to one side and confided in him that Busby and Tucker had been tampering with his tea bottle, and that Busby had torn his coat. Busby told Stone not to tell tales about him, presumably thinking that Stone had been speaking to Gilbert. When Stone told him that it was Gilbert who had been speaking to him, Busby called Gilbert a liar to his face and Gilbert flung back the accusation at Busby. The latter told Gilbert he would take the matter to the company and, if they refused to listen, to court. There was a row between Gilbert and Busby, neither man willing to back down on their already entrenched positions. Busby was ready with his fists and Gilbert raised a shovel as if to strike him, but the two did not come to blows.

Busby reported Gilbert to James Reed, the inspector on the Junction Railway, who supervised Gilbert's group and to whom Gilbert reported. The complaint was put down in writing. Reed announced that there would be a formal hearing on 28 August at Great Kimble station, in the presence of Mr J. Frome, Chief Clerk to the District Engineer. In the meantime, the men would have to continue working together, and were told that they must be on their best behaviour. Reed knew that Gilbert was not an easy character to work with and had been moved from sections in the past, and that Busby and Tucker were hard workers and men of good character.

When the day came for the hearing, Busby told Mr Frome that he had not damaged Gilbert's coat nor had he tampered with his tea, but he admitted that he had threatened to fight him. Mr Frome told him that he should not have done so and should have reported him instead. Busby added that Gilbert was peculiar, as he had suggested that he and Tucker were plotting against him whenever they conversed together. Gilbert said that Busby was late to work, disobedient and belligerent. He claimed that Busby had said to Tucker, 'You must swear false against Gilbert to get shot of him.' The decision as to what should happen next would be made in a few days time.

On Saturday 29 August, Tucker, who lived with his uncle Charles, a smallholder, rose at a quarter past five. He seemed well and healthy, and cycled to work at the railway station at about twenty to six. Busby probably left home before six, though his fellow lodger was asleep when he left. Percy Watson, a farm labourer of Great Kimble, set out for Chalkshire Farm, Ellesborough, where he worked. He saw Gilbert at about a quarter to six, leaving home for the railway station. Gilbert was carrying his stick, as he always did. The two men exchanged greetings. Gilbert's neighbour at number 4 was Herbert Howard, the stationmaster, who also saw him leaving at about this time.

However, at about half past six, Mr Howard saw Gilbert return home, but he left after another seven minutes. Howard himself arrived at the railway station at seven o'clock. There was no one else there.

At 7.15 a.m. Gilbert told PC Dillow of Ellesborough – who was still at home at that time – that he wished to confess to a double murder.

The scene of the crime was not attractive. In the cabin, which measured only 13ft by 9ft, were the two, still warm, bodies. Police Sergeant Hill searched the bodies but found nothing relevant, only personal belongings and certainly nothing which could be construed as a weapon. Nearby, however, was a pickaxe shaft and a shovel, both bloodstained, and the latter had human hairs attached. Thomas Rutland, another foreman platelayer on the railway, later found a bag and a keying hammer on the top of a nearby bridge. These belonged to Gilbert.

PC Dillow contacted Superintendent Henry Wootton at Aylesbury, who arrived to take charge. When he arrived, he saw that Gilbert was about to make a statement. He took him to one side and made sure that the man realised the enormity of what he had done. Gilbert said that he did and made the following statement:

> My name is Thomas Gilbert and I reside at No. 3 Icknield Cottages, Little Kimble, and am a foreman platelayer on the Great Western and Great Central Railway. My length extends from the station to a mile the other side of Marsh Crossing. I am married and have three children. I have got two men in my section. Their names are Charles Busby and Walter Tucker. Yesterday we had an official inquiry, through Busby wanting to fight me, but I have never struck him. After the inquiry yesterday I heard Busby say, 'I shall get a revolver'. He said that two or three times. He has threatened two or three times that he would do me in. He also told a man some time ago that he would put me over. The man was Wyatt, of Smoky Row, Great Kimble. At 6.15 this morning, Saturday August 29th, Charles Busby came into the cabin where I was. I had some suspicion that he had the revolver, which he had spoken about before. Being suspicious, I went for him and knocked him over with a pick shaft. The other man (Tucker) tried to hold me but I knocked him over, also with the same weapon. I don't think I killed either. I then went and informed the police that I had knocked them over. I did not know whether I had killed them. I got to my cabin at 6 o'clock and Tucker arrived directly after me.

Dr Max Onslow-Ford, from Wendover, arrived on the scene and, upon examining the bodies, declared that he thought the men had been dead for two to three hours, as there was no sign of rigor mortis having set in. Their clothes were not damaged, however, Tucker's head had been badly battered, with a depression being found in the skull, and the face had been flattened; the nose pushed back, with blood flowing from the nose and ears. The forehead was also bruised. Busby had also taken a blow to the head and there were several wounds to the forehead. There was no sign of a struggle. In both cases, the cause of death was the same: 'A compound complicated fracture of the skull and extensive cerebral haemorrhage.' Tucker had died immediately; Busby some minutes after the attack.

That afternoon, the inquest was opened at The Crown pub by Mr S.E. Wilkins, deputy county coroner. Joseph Tucker, a farm labourer, identified the corpse of his brother, and recalled last seeing him alive on the Friday evening before the murders. He could not recall his brother telling him about any ill feeling among his workmates. Charles Busby, a plumber and house decorator, identified his brother. After that, the coroner adjourned the inquest for a week. Later that

Baptist church, Kimble.

day, Gilbert was brought before the Magistrates' Court and was charged with murder. Superintendent Wootton outlined the arrest of the prisoner and his statement was read out in court. Gilbert was remanded in prison for a week.

In the meantime, both Busby and Tucker were buried, one after a service in the Baptist church, the other at the parish church. Both services were well attended by the friends, families and workmates of the two young men; both of whom seemed to be popular and sadly missed, judging by the amount of people in attendance and the number of wreaths. Meanwhile, many people had taken a great interest, or a morbid curiosity, in the cabin where the murders took place.

The inquest was reconvened on 4 September at The Crown, and lasted for four hours. Gilbert wore a black coat and black corduroy trousers, but lacked a collar or tie. He clasped and unclasped his hands incessantly, and took a keen interest in the proceedings. A great number of witnesses gave their accounts of the events leading up to the murders. Eliza Webb, Tucker's fiancée, reported that he had told her that Gilbert was of a funny disposition, and that he and Busby hoped Gilbert would leave soon and that they would have a new foreman over them. A letter from Busby was read out, which said that Gilbert had reported Busby for smoking whilst at work – which he had – but that he had been working as well, and that Gilbert had threatened to sack him. The jury inevitably concluded that this was a case of wilful murder by Gilbert.

Much of the same evidence was given before the Magistrates' Court on the following day, with the result that Gilbert was committed for trial at the next Buckinghamshire Assizes. In the meantime, he was sent to Oxford Prison.

The trial took place at Aylesbury on 13 October, resided over by Sir Horace Avory. Mr MacCardie led the case for the prosecution, while Gilbert was defended by the renowned Sir Ryland Adkin, KC, MP.

As ever, in cases of this type, when there was no doubt that the accused had committed murder, the defence was one of insanity, which could result in the accused escaping the death penalty. Clearly, the prosecution disagreed with such a notion, and pointed to Gilbert's cool nature, even just after he had committed murder. If he was sane, as he appeared, and he really believed that he was threatened by Tucker and Busby, resulting in their murder, he must be found guilty.

Albert Stone was the first witness to appear for the prosecution and he gave evidence of seeing Gilbert on the morning of the murder. Reed spoke next, stating that the two men had known each other since about 1903, when they had worked together in Nottingham on a daily basis. James Reed said that Gilbert was intelligent, as he would have to be to hold a responsible position in the railway company. He was also a good and precise workman. He then read out the contents of a letter that he had received from Gilbert earlier in the year:

Dear Sir,

I wish to report C. Busby to you, sir, for standing about smoking, and not getting on with his work. When I spoke to him, he said, 'H_ to you' 2 or 3 times. I asked him to get ready to put the loading sack in after the 9.33 a.m. and he said he was not going to hurry himself for me, and kept on standing instead.

Your obedient servant, T. Gilbert

This was not the first time that Gilbert had felt that he was being threatened by his fellow workers, however, and Reed read out an earlier letter:

Haddenham July 1910

Dear Sir,

I wish to report to you that I spoke to E. Parker this morning, July 2 1910, for being late. I said, 'Come on, my man. This won't do. You want to get here in your time.' He said, 'What the b_ h_ is it to do with you? I will chop your b_ head off with my shovel if you speak to me.' I said, 'My man, time is time. I want nothing but what is reasonable.' It is not the first time that this man has threatened to strike me on the head with his tools, so I think it high time to inform you before anything happens. Yours obediently, T. Gilbert

Apparently, in 1912, Elijah Parker was accused by Gilbert of putting poison in his food and drink. Gilbert's letter recounted what action he took:

I went to Dr Cooke, of Haddenham, to be examined, and told him I was of [the] opinion a man had been putting poison in my drink. I asked him to examine me and told him how my tongue has been sore underneath.

In order to keep the peace, the railway company moved Gilbert to Kimble, but this did not solve the problem. Mr Reed did not believe there was any sign of insanity in Gilbert at this time, though he was hardly medically qualified to hold such a view.

In September 1912, Gilbert had sent a bottle of cocoa, which he believed had been poisoned, to be examined by the company's chemist, but no trace was found.

Other witnesses called for the prosecution included the police officers who had seen Gilbert on the day of the murder. A doctor also told the jury that, of the assaults made by Gilbert, in both cases there was much more violence used than was necessary to kill. This completed the case for the prosecution.

The defence argued that Gilbert did not know right from wrong – though he was responsible for the two deaths, he was not morally guilty. A number of doctors were summoned to give their opinions. The first was Dr Richard Harvey Sankey, Medical Officer at Oxford Prison, who had had plenty of opportunity to observe Gilbert whilst he had been detained there. He concluded that he was of unsound mind. He recollected that Gilbert was happy to talk about the case, but he was certain that since 1911 he had been poisoned by various men. He suffered from delusions, even though on arrival he had seemed calm, cool and collected. He would be happy to certify him as a lunatic. Another doctor summoned by the defence was Dr Thomas Saxby Good, Medical Superintendent of Oxfordshire County Lunatic Asylum. He had seen Gilbert on 10 October and he too confirmed that Gilbert was of unsound mine, and that he had been suffering from delusions and making rambling and incoherent statements.

The defence summed up that Gilbert was suffering from mental delusions and was unable to be held responsible for his actions. The prosecution reminded the jury that he had been able to carry out his duties as a railway employee and as a husband, so was responsible and, therefore, guilty. The judge summed up the case for half an hour, pointing out to the jury that this was not a case of manslaughter, but murder, and he defined how the law saw the difference between insanity and sanity. He said that if a man believes another is attacking him and he defends himself, the former's behaviour is acceptable, but if he only believed that a man bears him a grudge and so may attack him in the future, and he then attacks him as a pre-emptive strike, then that is not permissible. The jury left the court for only fifteen minutes before returning with their verdict. They found that the accused man was guilty. Gilbert was then asked by the judge if he had anything to say. Often the prisoner has nothing to say, but in this case, Gilbert was voluble:

> It stands for me to speak. You listened to statements made here tonight of three men working together. One could tell a lie and the other could swear false to it and it is that that is bringing this thing to what it has done. That has brought me here, but I shall speak the truth. Charles Busby told the lie and Walter Tucker swore to it. That has brought us here today. We have been told – one has told the lie, and the other swore to it. I will tell say this: I paid twenty-four shillings to the police to have it analysed, on suspicion it was tampered with . . . I am very sorry I have not had a chance to speak and defend myself.

He concluded with a pronouncement from the Lord's Prayer. His voice then dropped and he finished with, 'I don't know what I want to say anymore.' The judge then handed down the death sentence and Gilbert stumbled down the steps of the dock to the cells, to be returned to prison.

In earlier times, this would have been the end of the case, but in 1907 the Court of Appeal had been founded, and Messrs Robert Samuel Wood, solicitors of High Wycombe, who had been handling the case out of court, made an appeal to this court on Gilbert's behalf, on the grounds that the judge had misdirected the jury. The case was held by a panel of judges on 3 November. As before, Adkins and McCardie appeared. They decided that Gilbert was insane at the time he committed his murders, and therefore quashed the sentence and instead directed that he be sent to an asylum, presumably Broadmoor. The 1883 Lunatics Act stated that a man can be sent to an asylum if a verdict of 'guilty but insane' was given. The solicitors were congratulated on being the first to win an appeal from the Court of Criminal Appeal. It is not known how long Gilbert remained in an asylum, but he is recorded as having died in Basford, Nottinghamshire, in 1938.

Thomas Gilbert was probably suffering from what we would now term paranoid schizophrenia, for he was imagining things which did not exist, and his otherwise unjustified violence sprang from these delusions. These signs were evident from 1910, when he accused Elijah Parker of having designs on his life, but his employers, clearly not realising their significance, did not properly deal with them.

13

'I HAVE BEEN A SOURCE OF WORRY AND TROUBLE'

Little Marlow, 1921

Women's rights took a massive step forward in the year of 1918. It is well known that women aged thirty or over were now allowed to vote in General Elections; however, what is less well-known is that women were also allowed to perform jury duty for the first time. This chapter focuses on the first murder case in which women were jury members.

Little Marlow, a couple of miles to the east of Marlow, is not a large village. It is certainly not the sort of place where serious crime is commonplace. Yet, in 1920, the conclusion to a murky tale of domestic intrigue occurred there. Two newly arrived residents were George Arthur Bailey, a dairyman, and Kate Lilian Bailey, his wife. They had one child. Their antecedents were surely little known to their new neighbours.

Bailey had been born on 13 March 1888 in West Hampstead. He was the fourth and youngest son of George and Betsy Bailey. He initially worked as an office boy at Messrs Lochart, a coal merchant, in Cricklewood and then as a grocers' boy until 1905. His father died that year in Hampstead Workhouse, suffering from religious mania. This may have had cataclysmic results for his son; for it was then that his future took a downward turn.

Nothing much is known of his next three years, but he worked on farms in Leicestershire in 1906, and was sentenced at Northampton for four offences of fraud and forgery on 10 June 1908. He was given a sentence of twenty months in gaol with hard labour. He then went to Devonshire and was again employed on a farm. In 1913, he was employed by the Express Dairy Company in London as a milkman, but in June of that year he absconded with money he had embezzled. Later that year he was arrested in Exeter and was given six months with hard labour. Trouble was never far away from this young man.

In June 1916 he was released from prison and joined the Devonshire Regiment. He deserted two months later. On 12 August 1916 he married eighteen-year-old Kate Lilian Lowden, at Lambeth Registry Office. Little is known about Kate, except that she was later described by neighbours as a timid little woman, devoted to her husband. But Bailey's criminal career continued, being wanted for larceny and forgery in August of the following year. At a Torquay lodging house in the same month he stole £11 10s. He and his wife absconded and fled to London, where he stole some jewellery and a chequebook. The law caught up with him on 13 November 1917 when he was charged with forgery and larceny. A Hampshire court sentenced him to three years imprisonment, and his wife, who had acted as his accomplice in helping him clear cheques, six months – she gave birth to a daughter whilst in Winchester Prison.

Bailey was released from Parkhurst Prison on the Isle of Wight on 6 February 1920 on licence (meaning he could be immediately recalled to prison if he committed any offences). Bailey, his wife and daughter then lived at 19 Perry Street, Swindon, with Bailey's sister and his brother-in-law, the Jennings. They left Swindon in April, but returned in June, then left again. This time, Bailey took up a milkman's job with Mr Hall's dairy at The Parade, Bourne End, having answered an advert in *The Farmer and Stockbreeder* in May. Hall met him in Wallingford and hired him, perhaps because of his previous experience on farms and as a milkman. He was described as being abstemious, decent, steady and energetic. A former employer had given him a good reference. On 29 May he began working for £3 a week, plus commission. He did well, and had 300 customers on his round. He sold forty dozen eggs per week and a cwt of butter per month, and he earned commission on these sales. He was popular, and his weekly wage was raised by five shillings.

It should be noted that Bailey's early life was not an unrelieved one of criminality. He had suffered from ill health throughout his life. He had been forced to give up his first job due to sickness, and had been an inmate in Banstead Asylum between February and June 1911. In the same year he had made two unsuccessful suicide attempts; he also took an overdose of opium and laudanum in 1917, in Winchester. He had also written poems and plays, but none of the latter had been published, though it had been commended. Bailey himself was described as a clean-shaven man of rather less than medium stature and with somewhat heavy features.

Bailey was more than a milkman, however. He considered himself musically talented, and though he did not know a single note of music, he was convinced that he had invented a new system of sheet music notation. Not all shared his beliefs; Dr Samuel Bath of Marlow, a doctor of music, considered Bailey's method to be grotesque and likened it to drawings of tadpoles seeking an incubator, to which Bailey responded, 'It is not a grotesque absurdity, but the fruits of hard study.' He sought assistants and had been placing adverts in the local newspaper in order to encourage well-built young women, aged sixteen or more, to visit his cottage. They were there, apparently, to take music lessons with a view to performance. He offered them £5 5s per week.

The first advert was placed in the *Buckinghamshire Free Press* in June 1920, and it read:

> Young lady, refined, educated, musical ability essential, required to help originator copy manuscript proof sheets, and assist in development of propaganda. Pleasantly unique work: light hours. Salary five guineas, weekly to right person. Write, GAB, 'FP' Office, Wycombe.

It is presumed that either no one replied or Bailey found the applicants unsatisfactory for, two months later, a similar advert appeared in the same paper:

> Young ladies, not under sixteen, must be five feet six inches tall, well built, full figure or slim build. Applicants below height specified please state qualifications as to appearance, etc. Required for highly paid, specialised work, indoors or out. Applications from all classes entertained, as duties will be light. Write, in first instance, to 'Snap', 'FP' Office, Wycombe.

Miss Lilian Victoria Roas Marks, a twenty-year-old grocers' assistant, arrived at Millbrook – Bailey's house – on 6 September. Bailey asked her about her musical ability and she answered that she had little. She was also asked to remove her coat to display her figure. Bailey explained his new musical system and offered to pay her £3 3s per week. He said he planned to form a school of seven or eight pupils under his instruction. Miss Marks told Bailey that she would need to give her current employer notice, and also have her parents approve of the situation. On 10 September he wrote and asked her to return to his house in Little Marlow.

At the same time, Bailey had also been on the quest for poison. This had once been relatively easy to obtain, but now it was only in the hands of chemists and doctors. He had began by asking Miss Parsons, a photographer's assistant, for prussic acid on the basis he needed it to destroy wasps' and ants' nests. He was turned down. Then, on 20 September, he asked Mr Hancocks of Messrs Zimmerman and Co., Wholesale Chemists, for devotal for human and animal use. Bailey claimed to be a veterinary surgeon and asked for other drugs, too; but only devotal was supplied. Another firm was applied to for prussic acid, but Bailey's order was refused. Finally, not being able to buy what he wanted from a London supplier, he tried locally, and met Stanley King, a Marlow chemist. On 28 September, he bought chloroform, opium and prussic acid from him, signing the poisons book in front of witnesses.

Bailey had been off work from 15 September, alleging sickness, and his employer had paid Mrs Bailey her husband's sick pay on 27 September. He claimed his lungs were unwell, and had an abscess in his face.

Relations between husband and wife that autumn were not good. Mrs Eliza Hesther of the post office thought the two always lived on good terms, claiming that Bailey, 'Was always speaking about his dear wife, and was loud in his praise of her capabilities.' She was also six months pregnant. He bought her a gown in August, but she had not wanted it. She objected to the time and money he was spending on his musical schemes and she resented him inviting young women to their home. On 15 September, William Day had seen Bailey with his hand around Kate's throat, saying, 'My God, I will put an end to you,' though Bailey later denied this.

Saturday, 29 September 1920 was the last day of Kate's life. She was seen alive in the afternoon, but not after. It was also on this day that three candidates for the post of Bailey's assistant arrived at the cottage. These were Miss Edwards and Miss Field of Marlow – both aged sixteen – and Miss Lilian Marks. Miss Edwards and Miss Field arrived first and Bailey gave them a short musical lesson before discharging them for the remainder of the day. Miss Marks was told to go away, have lunch (which Bailey gave her four shillings for) and then to return at seven that evening. When she did so, she was told that the other two girls had journeyed down from Scotland and were so tired that, though in the cottage, they had gone to bed, and that another young lady would join them later that evening. These were untruths, but they encouraged Miss Marks to remain in the house, to have supper, and to be shown to a bedroom, the door of which lacked a lock. She went to bed at 9.30 p.m., but could not fall asleep. She could hear Bailey pacing about downstairs.

Bailey entered her bedroom that night, to ask her if she could hear his daughter crying. He then asked her why she could not sleep and she replied it was because of his presence. Bailey then said, 'What do you think of this cottage?' The girl replied, 'The cottage is alright, but I don't want to discuss it now.' Undeterred, Bailey continued, 'How would you like to be mistress of the cottage?' She repeated that she did not want to discuss the matter and asked him to leave. Bailey refused and sat on the bed next to the terrified girl. He then got into the bed, presumably for the purpose of sex; she resisted him, to the extent that she suffered bruises all over her body, and tried to escape by getting to the window and shouting for help (Mrs Hesther later reported hearing two screeching sounds, but put them down to owls and did nothing). Miss Marks failed to escape but her honour remained intact.

The next morning, Bailey asked her if she would tell anyone what had happened, but she did not reply. He then told her that the previous night, no one would want to marry her, so she should consent to become the mother of his children. Bailey presented his daughter and said that her mother was unwell and in Swindon. Miss Marks asked for breakfast, which was given to her, and she ate while Bailey shaved. He then asked her if she wanted a music lesson, but she was too upset to answer. Finally, he asked her to take some money and buy specified foods in the village for him, which she did.

Miss Fields and Miss Edwards arrived at 11.30 a.m. as planned, and Miss Marks showed them in, before leaving and walking to Cores End. The two girls remained with Bailey for only an hour and he asked them to return at eight o'clock that evening. Reverend Allan then called on Bailey that afternoon to ask what had happened to Miss Marks, who had called on the reverend and made a complaint against Bailey before returning home to her parents. Bailey replied unhelpfully, 'Marks? Marks? I don't remember the name of Marks.'

Bailey left the cottage that evening and the two girls came back to an empty house. He arrived at the Jennings' in Swindon and told them his wife was about to give birth in High Wycombe Hospital. They believed him. The next day he returned to the cottage in Little Marlow, but was back in Swindon in the evening, telling his relatives that his wife had died in hospital. That day he also sent a telegram to Miss Edwards and Miss Fields, asking them to appear at the cottage on the next day.

Based on information recieved from either Reverend Allan or Miss Marks' parents, the police became involved on 2 October, when Superintendent George Kirby of High Wycombe and Inspector William West, of Marlow, called at the cottage at nine in the morning. There was no response, so the Inspector entered by an open window and then let his superior in through the door. On the dining room table was found the remains of a meal, with bread, butter, cake, buns, milk pudding and jam laid out. They searched the premises and quickly found the corpse of Mrs Bailey, wrapped in a sheet and under a camp bed. Doctors Francis Hugh Pougall Wills and John Dunbar Dickson, medical partners of Marlow, were called. They pronounced her dead, due to poisoning.

A letter from Mrs Bailey was found. It read:

Mother, will you take care of my little Hollie for me, or see she is taken care of; I can't stand it any longer. Stand what, you will want to know. I am not going to say anything, George can tell you all. I don't know if it is me to blame; it always is, so I expect it is me again. Never mind, it is nothing new. It is a shame you are called upon when anything goes wrong; it will be the last time where I am concerned, for I shall take jolly good care it is the last time. If I only knew Hollie would be looked after, I would not care a hang, and George would not mind if he never saw me again. I am alright to get his food for him, look after the kiddie, but otherwise I am? Oh mother, it hurts too much to be told that what I have, what we both have been through together, I am not so strong as I used to be; God knows I have had it all taken out of me, the shame, the disgrace of it all. Can you wonder why I feel quiet, want to dress quiet, want to keep away from everybody; I can't always forget, even if George can.

By now, Bailey had left his daughter at Swindon with the Jennings and caught the train to Reading. He sent the two girls more telegrams, asking them not to arrive as previously requested, due to a death occurring at the cottage. That evening, Bailey was arrested outside Reading station by PC Poole, from Marlow, and DS Purdy, from Reading. On his person were numerous bottles. These contained various poisons, including prussic acid, opium, chloroform and stramonia. He was also carrying fifteen shillings. There was also a letter, apparently explaining his actions. It read:

Please do not worry my people; please do not worry her people. There is no need to divulge where I come from or divulge that I belong to so and so, for my dear mother's and brother's and sister's sake. There is no need to call any witnesses for evidence. This is the final act of an unbalanced, yet vigorous brain. My darling is waiting for me. I gave her here my child first. Then I follow the same death that she died. I handed the poison to her, she believed my statements, they are our secrets. I pray God he lets us be united as we have always believed we should be. She is asking for me, for her child now. I have contemplated horrible things, almost accomplished them. Please take great care of the music I leave behind, it is the notation of the future, if only the old school would overcome their jealousies, their conservatism, their prejudices. I have shown several young ladies its simplicity. Miss Fields, Miss Edwards, and Miss Marks can explain more.

I heard my darling die on Wednesday 29th September at 7.15 pm. I have waited my fate and now I meet it. My own dear wife knows and knew, but she is so brave, so staunch, that God will forgive her. Forgive me. Please do not let this tragedy destroy the future of this notation, but that someone with foresight will take it up. I ask for no pardon from the world. I have even been a source of worry and trouble. It has been harder to fight than I can resist and I have tried, but I know and knew that it must all end in some such way.

I should like our three bodies to be laid together, that is why I came back to take one last look; give one last kiss to my beloved. I gave her stramonia first, then hydrocyene. No blame attaches to the chemist. I could always bluff to attain my ends. Goodbye my dear mother, my own dear sister, Nellie, and brother-in-law Jim. Wayward when young, but easily to be corrected if they had only known. I believe I have been broken-hearted since poor dad died and I failed to make good, but my own beloved darling wife Kitty understood me and loved me so much. Yes, in my own way, my life has been given to her no matter what I intended to do. It was always decided to go together and not to leave our baby behind. Please God, Father of all Nature, forgive us all, but I do believe in thy existence as more simple than the Bible is taught, just our father who must recognise him in such.
My darling I am coming.

Bailey was taken to Reading police station and was questioned by Inspector West. On 4 October, Bailey was charged at Marlow Magistrates' Court with the murder of his wife.

An inquest was opened on the following day and he was remanded in custody. Public responses to Bailey were unfavourable and crowds booed him on his way to the court. The inquest was adjourned and not concluded until 26 November. In the interim, Dr Bernard Spilsbury, the well-known Home Office pathologist, and his colleague, Dr Webster, conducted the post-mortem and found that prussic acid was the cause of death. Bailey was found to be the guilty party, though had already been remanded for trial.

Whilst Bailey was held by the police, he made a statement to one PC Gray:

Between me and you, Kit and I were in the garden Wednesday evening. About 5pm, we went indoors, and had tea, some buns, and bread and butter. Her last words to me

The former Magistrates' Court, Marlow.

were, 'You will have to come too.' We were very loving to one another. I had already made my mind up what to do, although I am an atheist, it came across my mind that we should be parted forever. On Thursday evening, I locked the front door, took the child and put the key through the letterbox and went off. My intentions were to come back to Little Marlow on Saturday. I done wrong in telling them at Swindon that my wife was at Wycombe Hospital. It has made it look black against me. I should have made a clear statement to Inspector West, but as it will not help court proceedings, I shall keep quiet. If this goes against me, I wish all my things at Barn Cottage shall be burnt, except the pushchair, and I want that to be given to our little girl.

Bailey was incarcerated in Oxford Prison, where he was a model prisoner. He read the newspapers, sketched, wrote poetry and amended his musical notation.

He was put on trial at the county assizes at Aylesbury, starting on Thursday 13 January. Bailey was brought from Oxford Prison to Aylesbury, arriving just after ten. He was accompanied by two warders and seemed in good spirits. Mr Wood of High Wycombe was his solicitor. There were many sightseers, but the trial did not commence until 2.25 p.m. Bailey pleaded 'not guilty'.

On Friday 14 January, the defence began, saying that Kate had committed suicide by taking poison and Bailey was put in the witness box to attest to this.

He spoke for five hours in total. He declared that his wife was suffering from nervous depression and had tried to kill herself on two or three previous occasions. He explained that he had bought the poison because he wanted to set up in business as a veterinary surgeon. He had actually witnessed his wife's death; she had been seen in bed with an egg cup of poison and had said, 'Come too,' before falling back, dead. He was in the witness box from 12.30 until 6 p.m.

His statement, read out in court, was as follows:

I beg to emphatically deny both the charges [rape and murder] laid against me. I hope to prove that my purpose in obtaining these various drugs and medicines was for the purpose of taking up farrier work – not as a qualified veterinary surgeon – but for the purpose of raising money. That the cyanide of potassium was ordered for the purposes stated to Miss Parsons. I hope to prove that my system of the staff notation is all I claim for it, and that a grotesque absurdity it was not a farce, or a cloak for nefarious designs, but the fruits of hard study and investigation. That I did not commit felonious assault or rape on Miss Marks. That I did not threaten or assault my wife at Little Marlow. We were not there; that evidence is utterly false. That in the main the evidence of the prosecution is built upon unreliable facts and supposition. That I acted and thought throughout the whole period from my coming to Millbrook, to the taking of, and the living at Barn Cottage, in an abnormal simple story of love and devotion on both sides, hardships, trials surmounted, triumph within sight, then disaster and collapse.

As to what exactly happened on 29 September, we shall never know. Kate Bailey was seen alive in her the garden in the afternoon by a neighbour, but was clearly dead by the time Miss Marks arrived at the cottage that evening. We know she had died by taking prussic acid, but we only have Bailey's word for what actually happened. He claimed that he saw her on the couch, sitting up, with half a bottle of stramonia nearby. Her legs, arms and head were shaking. Bailey took her into the garden, walked her about and made her throw nuts onto the ground before collecting them. They then went indoors and he brought her some tea. She complained of experiencing unpleasant sensations, but then seemed to improve. She went up to the bedroom and, later, Bailey saw her in bed with the egg cup and an open bottle of prussic acid. Although he claimed he tried to revive her with chloroform, he was unsuccessful.

The novelty of three of the jury being female had practical consequences. Miss Maud Stevenson objected to being on a murder case, but was told that she had no choice in the matter. There were breaks in the proceedings in the afternoons, so that the jury could have a tea break. Defence counsel felt embarrassed at raising certain questions because there were ladies present, and hesitated in his execution of these. The judge had to remind him that,

> In this Court, there can be no such thing as delicacy if it interferes with the arriving at the truth. I am sure that the ladies on the jury will understand that when they take their place in the jury box, their sole duty is to arrive at the truth and give a proper verdict.

There had been an effort to conclude the trial on Friday 14 January, in order to release them from their duty before the weekend. This was not possible. Therefore, in order to prevent discussion of the case, they were obliged to stay at a local public house, The Bull, over the weekend, though they were allowed to attend a church service on Sunday. They were assigned a female usher. The trial was then concluded on the Monday with a guilty verdict being brought against Bailey. Donning the black cap, the judge sentenced him to death.

The following month, at the Court of Criminal Appeal, Mr Sinclair Johnston appeared for the appellant. He put forward that Bailey had not administered the poison which had killed Kate. Furthermore, the evidence for the alleged motive should not have been admitted. Mr Justice Avory dismissed the appeal

The Bull pub, near Aylesbury.

on the grounds that Bailey's evidence had been a mass of contradictions. He said that the only reasonable assumption could be that Bailey had bought the poisons which killed Kate, and that he had either given them to her himself, or at the very least, helped her to commit suicide. He also declared that evidence of motive was admissible; that Bailey had invited young women to come to his house and, having killed his wife, tried to assault Miss Marks under his roof on the same day. There was no question of Bailey being insane, and although the jury were allowed to return a verdict of guilty but insane, they did not do so.

On the day before his execution, Bailey's solicitors visited him. Instead of expressing any sense of injustice about his fate, he was calm, resigned and expressed concern about his daughter's future and his musical work, telling them, 'Don't let my music die.' At eight in the morning on Wednesday, 2 March 1921 he was hanged at Oxford Prison. He appeared cool as he walked the few steps to the gallows and his death.

14

A PUB SHOOTING

High Wycombe, 1937

Alcohol often plays a role in crimes of violence, as it fires passions which are already there, presumably latent, and this case is no exception.

Major Robert George Rhodes Godby and his wife, Katherine May Godby, had lived in High Wycombe since the late 1920s. In 1921, he became a Flying Officer with the RAF, entering the Reserve in 1925, but had left in 1930. He married Katherine, who was a year younger than her husband, in London, in 1929. They did not have any children. From September 1936 until 19 March 1937 they went on a trip to New Zealand. On their return they lived at 38 Mill End Road, in the Sands suburb of High Wycombe, in a house belonging to Albert Edward Green and his wife. The Greens, and Mrs Green's unemployed brother, lived at the same house with them.

Albert Boddy, was born in High Wycombe in 1905, the youngest of seven children of a cane framer. By 1937 he was bricklayer and lived with his married sister, Elizabeth Cook, and her husband, Levi Cook, at 62 Lane End Road, Sands, High Wycombe. He was single and had no savings. He was also a poacher and had four convictions already; one as recently as 20 March 1937, when he was found guilty of shooting pheasants on Sir John Dashwood's land and had his gun confiscated. He was also a friend of the Godbys and they regularly met each other in the Hour Glass public house in Sands, where Mrs Godby liked to play darts and dominoes with the regulars. This pub was only a few minutes walk from where Boddy and the Godbys lived.

It is uncertain what the precise relationship between Boddy and Mrs Godby was. He stated that he loved her, but we don't know how far she reciprocated this. They certainly spent time in each other's company but this does not suggest anything more than friendship on her part. They had known each other for about a year, though most of this period had been spent apart when the Godbys were in New Zealand. Possibly, he read more into this friendship than was meant.

At lunchtime of Saturday, 27 March 1937, Ernest Bates, a chair maker, George Frederick, Mrs Godby and William Brooks were playing dominoes. Boddy was also present. A game was arranged for the evening. Boddy made the arrangements; he and Mrs Godby were to be partnered against Leslie Hill and Albert Green, with Bates as scorer. However, this arrangement was changed by Boddy, and oddly enough he was annoyed, 'What is the idea of you not wanting to partner me?'

That afternoon, Boddy went poaching with George Alloway. That evening, the Godbys, the Greens and Boddy were in the pub. Boddy left his sister's house and arrived between 6.10 and 7 p.m. He recalled,

> I went to the Hour Glass public house and Mrs Godby was there when I got there. Four of us, Mrs Godby, William Quarterman, Albert Green and myself, played shove half penny for about an hour. I then had a few drinks and sat talking and in between played darts and other games.

All this may seem normal enough, but Boddy was annoyed. He said to Ernest Bates, 'You have done it alright for me. She has got another client now and she does not want anything to do with me.' Bates replied, reasonably enough, 'I only told her what you told me to tell her; and I can soon put that right for you.'

It does not seem that there was any argument between Boddy and Mrs Godby. She had asked him to take part in the game, but then did not take much notice of him. Something did pass between them, but he would not say what; 'There was something she had said to me but no one will ever know. I shan't let her down. I shall not tell.'

Between half past nine and ten o'clock, Boddy left the pub and went to his lodgings, taking with him his nephew's gun. He told his sister – who saw him with it – that he had an argument to settle. She asked for it to be given to her, 'You are not going out with that. It does not belong to you,' and was concerned that the police might confiscate it. The gun was returned, and she asked him to stay at home for his supper, but he replied, 'I will be back in a minute for supper.' She noted that he was sober; 'He had had a drink but was not drunk.'

He then went to 34 Lane End Road, only 124 yards from the Hour Glass pub.

The Hour Glass pub, Sands.

He woke Mrs Gray and asked if he could borrow their gun from them, a weapon he had used before. He was given a 4.10 bore shotgun, which had a rusty barrel, and four cartridges from Mrs Gray's daughter-in-law, Mrs Agnes Ethel Gray, a thirty-four-year-old caretaker. They assumed he wanted the gun for poaching. The gun belonged to Frederick Gray, who had last used it the previous month and had subsequently reloaded it. Boddy then returned to the pub just before ten o'clock. William Rolfe, the licensee, called time. Albert Green went to fetch Mrs Godby's coat for her.

On his return, there was a loud sound of a gunshot. Mrs Godby received the full discharge of the shotgun in the centre of her face, fired at very short range. Boddy stood there and declared, 'I have done it. I will wait for the police.' He then threw the gun away, which was found behind the bar. William Rolfe later said, 'The first thing I saw was Boddy standing there with the gun broken, that was just inside the lobby and about halfway between the table and the entrance to the lobby.' Although Boddy had appeared sober, Rolfe added, 'There was a peculiar look about him. It might have been a dazed look. When I spoke to him he appeared to be very upset.' PC Leonard Peter Latter was near the pub when he was told of the shooting. He entered the pub and asked where the shooter was. Boddy had made no attempt to escape and immediately gave himself up. He told the policeman, 'I shot her, but I did not mean to kill her.'

Dr Joseph Murison Craig of Amersham Hill Lodge was told of the death at a quarter to eleven, and he arrived on the scene shortly afterwards. The doctor had attended the Godbys for the past five or six years. He saw that Mrs Godby had been shot between the eyes and the resulting haemorrhage had caused her death. Mrs Godby was taken to the War Memorial Hospital, High Wycombe, where she was pronounced dead on arrival.

In the meantime, an extremely upset Boddy was taken to High Wycombe police station, where he made the following statement:

> I went to the Hour Glass public house at Sands at about 6. 10 p.m. on 27 March, and Mrs Godby was there when I got there. Four of us, Mrs Godby, William Quarterman, Albert Green and myself played shove half penny for about an hour. I then had a few drinks and sat talking, and in between times played darts and other games. At about ten minutes to ten, I left the Hour Glass and spoke to Mrs Godby. As I did so, I walked home and got my gun to do some poaching. I looked into the Hour Glass. Mrs Godby was in the company of several other men, and on the impulse of the moment I got my gun out and shot her. I did not intend to kill her. I loved her. I only meant to kick up a row. I must have had too much to drink before. I made no attempt to escape.

Boddy was charged with murder at the Magistrates' Court at the Guildhall in High Wycombe on Monday 29 March. It was a brief hearing and Boddy was remanded in custody until 6 April. Mr William Thomas Jones, the Chief Constable, said that additional time was needed for the evidence to be collected and so informed the department of public prosecutions of this. Mr Allan James, Boddy's solicitor, had no objection to the remand, but asked that Boddy be granted a legal aid certificate. The chairman of the court, Councillor R.P. Clarke, who was also the Mayor, said that such would be granted. There was a further remand on 6 April. Boddy was housed at Oxford Prison in the interim. Crowds gathered outside the Guildhall on both occasions. They wished Boddy well, shouting, 'Keep a good heart', and 'Good luck, Bert.' Boddy seemed cheerful and recognised some of his relations among the onlookers.

The Guildhall at High Wycombe. (Courtesy of Paul Lang)

On 7 April, Mrs Godby was buried in a private funeral at the parish church of High Wycombe. Only her husband, sister and eight others were present when the vicar, Revd Charles Elliot Wigg, conducted the service. Often, funerals of those who have died violently attract large crowds, but in this instance, the details were kept secret.

The next hearing was held on 14 April. Mr Robey, Director of Public Prosecutions, recounted the case against Boddy. He suggested that there was a certain amount of deliberation on Boddy's part in his actions. Mr J.A. Flint, the defence counsel, claimed there was no case to go to trial, and that Mrs Godby's death was accidental. After all, Boddy had been friendly enough with her earlier that day when arranging a darts match for the evening. The magistrates retired for ten minutes, and on their return, Mr Clarke told the hearing that after careful consideration of Mr Flint's arguments, they found that there was a case for Boddy to answer and therefore would send him for trial. Boddy said, 'I plead not guilty and reserve my defence. I do not desire to give evidence or call witnesses.'

Boddy was tried at the next county assizes at Aylesbury on 20 May. Mr Paul Ernest Sandlands, KC, opened the case for the Crown. He said that Boddy and Mrs Godby had quarrelled and, as a result, Boddy left the pub, borrowed a gun

Aylesbury courthouse. (Courtesy of Paul Lang)

and shot her. Mr Flint argued that, 'This is a terrible accident which was never intended. At the worst there can only be a verdict of manslaughter.' Boddy spoke in his own defence and stressed it was all an accident; that he did not know the gun was loaded and did not intend to shoot Mrs Godby. The trial continued on the following day. Boddy was asked about his alleged jealousy that Mrs Godby had a preference for another man. He replied, 'She never did that, that I can say. She had often told me she was a bad woman for making me love her.'

Frederick Grey, the owner of the gun – which was unlicensed – declared that it had last been used on 27 February, when he used it in Sands Wood for rabbit shooting. He fired it and reloaded it soon afterwards. He had not removed the cartridge following cleaning the gun, and stated that he had left the gun loaded on two previous occasions.

The question was not whether Boddy had pulled the trigger of the gun that had killed Mrs Godby – clearly he had done that – but whether he had meant to kill her or not. If he was innocent, as he stated, then he must not have known that the gun was loaded, which was possible. If he was guilty, then he must have either loaded the gun himself, or knew that it was already loaded.

After forty minutes of discussion, the jury found Boddy guilty of manslaughter. Mr Justice Singleton agreed wholly with the jury, then sentenced Boddy to three years' penal servitude.

Boddy was certainly smitten with Mrs Godby, though the precise details are unknown. He certainly seems to have been annoyed with her, because he thought she preferred another man's company to hers. He sought to bring himself back to her notice in a most dramatic fashion by pointing the gun at her, though it is probable he did not know it was loaded and thus had not meant to shoot her, a move that proved fatal.

AFTERWORD

Murders committed in Buckinghamshire in the past are very unlike those depicted on the small screen in recent years. There is rarely much mystery about them at all, except in certain cases, such as the one in Slough in 1881 and in Bledlow in 1893, which were never solved; though it was suspicion, crucially, not evidence which strongly pointed to particular suspects. In others, the guilty party gave himself up or made no effort to escape arrest. There were some examples where the guilty party took a few days to be tracked down; as with John Owen in Reading in 1870. These were not detective mysteries as portrayed through drama, but real life.

Murder, judging by these cases, seems to have been a wholly male pastime, though victims are of both sexes, with a slight majority of women being killed compared to men, and in some cases children have been slain. Motivation varied from greed, to revenge or frustrated passion, or due to marital discord. Poisoning was rare and shooting a little more common. Blunt instruments and knives were more common tools of the killer; both being far readily available. Two killers were found to be insane. In half of these cases, the killer was executed; two were sent to prison, two to Broadmoor and a couple escaped scot free.

Although the cases recounted here are terrible indeed, we must recall that they were generally few and far between, and whole years could pass with a single one occurring. Most crimes do not result in fatalities, nor indeed in any violence. Yet it is the murders which are most memorable because they create more drama and greater intrigue for the local populace.

BIBLIOGRAPHY

Buckinghamshire Free Press (1921, 1937)

Buckinghamshire Herald (1873-1874, 1893, 1914)

Oxford Journal (1822)

Slough Observer (1881, 1900, 1910, 1912)

The Morning Chronicle (1822, 1828, 1830, 1870)

The Morning Post (1873)

The Times (1822, 1828, 1830, 1853-1854, 1870)

The Windsor and Eton Express (1853-1854)

Windsor, Eton and Slough Express (1881, 1910, 1912)

INDEX

Adkins, Ryland 112, 116, 134, 136
Aston Clinton 11, 16–17
Avery, John 91–2, 94–6
Avery, Richard 92, 95–6
Aylesbury 6–7, 11–12, 14–16, 18–19, 21,
    28–29, 34–6, 38–40, 49–50, 52, 55, 64,
    67, 76, 86, 115 127, 131, 145, 147, 153–4
Bailey, George 138–148
Bailey, Kate 138–9, 141–8
Berkhamsted 12, 14–15, 18–19
Bledlow 89, 92–3, 95, 156
Boddy, Albert 149–155
Brewerton, Benjamin 23, 25–7
Brooks, William 109–116
Buckingham 23–5
Burnham 43–4, 46–8, 52–3
Busby, Charles 129–134, 136

Colnbrook 81, 83, 97–8, 102
Croker, James 14, 16–22

Davis, Annie 117–128
Denham 57–60, 64–5, 67
Dorney 43
Dunham, Supt 60, 62–4, 68–9, 81, 83–5
Drake, Captain John Tyrwhitt 63

Edden, William 28–30, 33–40
Eton 43, 47, 49–50, 117–121, 123

Finmere 25

Gaddesden 12–14, 19, 22
Gilbert, Thomas 129–137
Godby, May 149–155
Godby, Major 149, 153
Goodwin, Ralph 43–6, 48–51, 54–5

Haddenham 29, 31–2, 34–5, 38, 134–5
Hatto, Moses 43–56
High Wycombe 7, 9, 60, 91–2, 94–5, 136,
    140, 142, 145, 149, 152–3

Kingham, Herbert 89–90, 94–5
Kingham, John 89–2, 94–6
Kirby, George, PS (later Superintendent) 119,
    142

Little Gaddesden 12, 18
Little Kimble 129–130, 132
Little Marlow 138, 140, 142, 146
London 8, 13–14, 19–21, 49, 63, 84, 103–4,
    109, 112, 116, 139

Marks, Inspector 117–118, 122
Marlow 138, 140–142, 145
Marshall, Emanuel 57–60, 63–4, 68–70
Mayne, Major Otway 108

Needle, Edward 11–12, 17, 22
Needle, Rachel 11–12, 16–17, 22
Nicholls, Hannah 71–6
Nicholls, Thomas 71–6

Olney 71–2, 75
Owen, John 61–4, 67–70, 81, 156
Oxford 19, 36, 95, 134–135, 145, 148, 152

Payne, Augustus 79–81, 83–8
Pearman, Supt 108, 112, 116, 118
Peate, Gustavus 103–4
Poyle 101

Radnage 89, 92–3, 95
Randall, Thomas 14, 16–22
Reading 62–3, 68, 109, 112, 116, 128,
    143–4, 156
Reville, Ann 79–88
Reville, Hezekiah 79–81, 83–8

Sedgwick, Eric James 117–128
Sewell, Solomon 37–42
Slough 6–7, 60, 62–3, 78–9, 81, 84, 86–7,
    105–116, 118–119, 122, 156

Smith, Lizzie 97–8, 100–101
Sturgeon, Mary Ann 43–56
Swindon 139, 142–3, 145

Thame 29, 34–5, 37, 40
Tingewick 23–6
Tring 13, 17–19
Tucker, Walter 129–134, 136
Tyler, Benjamin 37–42

Uxbridge 57–64, 67–70

Wells, William 23, 25–7
West, Inspector 142, 144–5
Williamson, Detective Supt Frederick 60
Wilson, Isabella 105–9, 111, 114–116
Windsor 84, 105–6, 108, 115

Yewsden Wood 89–91